D1527031

Liberalism and the Limits of Power

Liberalism and the Limits of Power

Juliet A. Williams

UGL
JC
574
.W5551
2005

First published in 2005 by
PALGRAVE MACMILLAN™
175 Fifth Avenue, New York, N.Y. 10010 and
Houndmills, Basingstoke, Hampshire, England RG21 6XS
Companies and representatives throughout the world.

PALGRAVE MACMILLAN is the global academic imprint of the Palgrave Macmillan division of St. Martin's Press, LLC and of Palgrave Macmillan Ltd. Macmillan® is a registered trademark in the United States, United Kingdom and other countries. Palgrave is a registered trademark in the European Union and other countries.

ISBN 1–4039–7103–X

Library of Congress Cataloging-in-Publication Data

Williams, Juliet.
    Liberalism and the limits of power / Juliet A. Williams.
        p. cm.
    Includes bibliographical references and index.
    ISBN 1–4039–7103–X
        1. Liberalism. 2. Political science—Philosophy. I. Title.

JC574.W555 2005
320.51—dc22   2005046273

A catalogue record for this book is available from the British Library.

Design by Newgen Imaging Systems (P) Ltd., Chennai, India.

First edition: November 2005

10 9 8 7 6 5 4 3 2 1

Printed in the United States of America.

For Ali, David and Roxana
With a love beyond words.

CONTENTS

ACKNOWLEDGMENTS

Originally I intended to call this book *Pushing Limits*, and though the title has changed, the underlying spirit has not. The phrase "pushing limits" aptly characterizes not just the substance of the argument in the following pages, but the process of writing it as well. Just as I have tried to push some of liberalism's central ideas beyond their usual scope, I have at times felt pushed to my own limits in writing the book. While life at the limit can be uncomfortable, it is always interesting, and fortunately for me, over the course of this project's development I have been inspired by a wonderful group of teachers, colleagues, and friends, all of whom dwell in one way or another on intellectual frontiers of their own.

Throughout my undergraduate and graduate school years, I was drawn to questions concerning the relationship between limits and liberty, and I have learned a great deal about this relationship from those teachers who provided me with much needed structure while also trusting me with my freedom. As an undergraduate, I was awed and inspired by Bonnie Honig, who first opened up the Pandora's box of liberalism's ambivalences to me. Thanks also to my undergraduate thesis advisor Michael Sandel, whose masterful ability to bring lucidity to complexity continues to amaze and humble me. In graduate school, I was fortunate to work with Isaac Kramnick, who teaches by example that there is always something new and profound to say about liberalism. I am grateful as well to Kathy Abrams for many useful and provocative conversations about feminism and political theory. It is a privilege to have had the opportunity to work with Ted Lowi, whose writing and teaching about the rule of law has deeply influenced my own thinking. Finally, I thank Andrew Rutten for being a most extraordinary advisor to me throughout graduate school and beyond.

I owe a very special debt to Keith Hjortshoj of the John S. Knight Writing Program at Cornell University. Writing is something all academics do, but rarely discuss. That is a shame, because learning about the experiences of other writers enlivens and humanizes the writing process. I thank Keith for helping me as I have struggled to bridge what sometimes felt like the infinite gap between mind and page. More recently, Jacqueline Stevens and David Hochman each have played the role of writing guru for me, and I thank them both for invaluable advice and support.

At the University of California, Santa Barbara, I am especially grateful to the members of the Law & Society Program and the Women's Studies Program for supporting me in this project, and for their many insights and helpful suggestions. I also thank Constance Penley for teaching me that doing scholarship is supposed to be fun, and Dick Hebdige for putting the humanity back into humanities scholarship. Over the years, I have had the opportunity to trade ideas with an extraordinary group of colleagues and friends, many of whom have read parts of this manuscript as it has developed. Thanks especially to Paul Apostolidis, Wendy Belcher, Pete Boettke, Jeff Friedman, Steven Gerenscer, Howard Gillman, Mary Hawkesworth, Nancy Hirschmann, Jim Johnson, Tim Kaufman-Osbourne, Chris Littleton, Alex Moon, Jeannie Morefield, Libbie Rifkin, Norm Rosenberg, Doug Usher, Elizabeth Wingrove, and Mark Yellin. I owe a special debt to Jeremy Varon, who first helped give life to so many of the ideas found within these pages. Finally, it truly has been a pleasure to work with my editor Toby Wahl at Palgrave Macmillan, and I thank the anonymous reader for exceptionally helpful comments on the original manuscript.

My family has been unfailingly encouraging as I have worked on this project over the years. I am grateful to my mother for teaching me that there isn't a problem in this world, intellectual or otherwise, which isn't helped by taking a step back and getting a pedicure. I thank my father and Amy for encouraging me no matter what to find the path that is for my steps alone. I thank as well my siblings and their families, who are an incredible source of strength and good humor in everything I undertake. I owe my deepest debt of gratitude to my husband, Ali Behdad, who made the completion of this book, and so much else in my life, possible. No stranger to pushing limits himself, Ali has helped me push through quite a few limits of my own. Wise yet open-minded, grounded but adventurous, Ali seduced me back into the life of the mind by showing how fulfilling it can be when shared with such an extraordinary companion.

I have often heard colleagues liken the process of completing a book to the act of giving birth. I have never been entirely comfortable with this comparison, but perhaps the two endeavors are not completely unrelated, as I finally finished this book not long after the birth of our son David, and not long before the birth of our daughter Roxana. To be sure, for their tender years they already have taught me a lifetime of lessons about pushing limits—and not just when it comes to matters like cookie allowances or bedtime—but by hurtling me into domains of wonder, delight, and love that far exceed anything I've known before.

CHAPTER ONE

Limited Government in the Liberal Tradition

In the United States, the close of the twentieth century will be remembered as a time of popular revolt against big government. Skillfully playing to a public mood of distrust, the Republican Party won a stunning victory in the Congressional elections of 1994, threatening the end of the era of political viability for politicians associated with welfare state initiatives having origins in the New Deal. Throughout the 1990s, many of the most successful candidates for office organized their campaigns around a seemingly oxymoronic strategy—running *for* public office by running *against* government. Following the Republican victory, the so-called New Democrats scrambled to update their image. Leading the charge, a resilient President Bill Clinton reversed course after the humiliating defeat of his ambitious national health care initiative, and was soon to be heard issuing the proud declaration that "the era of big government is over."[1] The ease with which Clinton executed his about face—effortlessly appropriating Republican antigovernment rhetoric—stands as a powerful testament to the profoundly bipartisan nature of public suspicion of government in the United States. Throughout the 1990s, while conservatives denounced high taxes, gun control, and environmental regulations, progressives engaged in a fight against big government of a different sort, galvanizing opposition to such policies as the War on Drugs, the death penalty, and reproductive rights restrictions. In the early years of the twenty-first century, the rhetoric of big government has receded from the headlines, but there is no sign that underlying public anxiety about governmental coercion has diminished. For those worried about the growth of government, "privacy" has become the watchword of the day as popular opposition spreads to policies ranging from the curtailment of civil liberties authorized by the USA Patriot Act of 2001 to federal policies facilitating the acceleration of the corporate collection of personal data, including medical and financial information.

How seriously should we take recent furors over the growth of government? Political scientist Theodore Lowi contends that perennial paroxysms of antigovernment sentiment in the United States for the most part are nothing more than a "purely ritualistic public dialogue," a knee-jerk reaction that in modern times has been superseded at all levels but the rhetorical by an underlying commitment to "the principle of positive government."[2] Noting that despite pledges to the contrary, the coercive power of government in the United States always seems to grow—even under the stewardship of outspoken opponents of big government like Reagan and the Bush presidents—Lowi suggests that the recent frenzy over big government is largely an exercise in symbolic politics. Lowi is certainly correct that there is nothing new about popular protestations against governmental intervention in the United States, where antigovernment rhetoric is as American as apple pie.[3] Since the very inception of the United States, popular uneasiness about the growth of government has been nourished by uncertainty concerning the ways to determine the appropriate scope and reach of government. Though some in the public may take heart in the assumption that the U.S. Constitution contains decisive answers to the question "how much government is too much," this comforting fiction is sustained by a lack of familiarity with the text of a document Americans may generally revere but rarely read. And it is undeniably the case that many of those who condemn the idea of big government as a matter of principle, nonetheless become advocates of interventionist legislation when doing so promises to advance their own agenda. It is tempting, then, to dismiss as mere hypocrites those Republicans who, for example, oppose taxation to support public schools but favor rules which compel students to recite the Pledge of Allegiance before class each day, or similarly, those Democrats who favor big government programs like single-payer health care but fret over the threat to privacy posed by the creation of a national medical records database. But behind these inconsistencies lies significant, and understandable, confusion about where and how to draw the line between public power and private rights. Scratch beneath the surface of the absolutist rhetoric espoused by both the political right and the left in the United States, and one finds a dense web of tangled views about the appropriate role for government to play in a liberal democratic society. When it comes to the question of limited government, the U.S. public is like the captain of ship who sailing with neither a map nor a compass is nonetheless convinced the boat has strayed off course.

Ongoing debate concerning the appropriate scope and reach of government attests, in part, to the constitutive role played by Anglo-American liberal political thought in shaping the terms and priorities of public discourse in the United States. Today, the word "liberal" has multiple meanings, and the label is as likely to be associated with the political documentaries of filmmaker Michael Moore as it is with the economic thought of the eighteenth-century Scottish philosopher Adam Smith. To understand liberalism's multiple meanings in contemporary colloquial usage, it is useful to trace the origins of the word itself. The term first appeared in the English language in the fourteenth century, used to describe those leisure activities "considered worthy of a free man."[4] In early usage, the term liberal also carried the connotation of one who is "free in bestowing" and "open-hearted." In time, the idea of a liberal as one who gives amply, or freely, gave way to the image of the liberal as one who acts "free from restraint," leading to the longstanding association between liberalism and imprudence or even immorality, as well as a connotation not just of excessive giving but "licentiousness" as well. In the nineteenth century, the meaning of the term evolved to include not just those considered to be "open-hearted," but those considered "open-minded" as well, in the sense of being free of prejudice. As a political ideology, the term liberalism rose to prominence in the nineteenth century to describe members of the British Parliament "favourable to constitutional changes and legal or administrative reforms tending in the direction of freedom or democracy," in contrast to conservatives, who sought to maintain the status quo. In modern day popular political parlance in the United States, the term liberal has become inseparable from its commonplace modifier "bleeding heart," and the label liberal is now a common term of derision for those left-of-center politicians who favor a government that is interventionist with respect to economics, but laissez-faire with respect to the legislation of morals.

Liberalism's divergent and perpetually evolving strains of meaning are reflected in the long and heterogeneous tradition of liberal political thought, a philosophical orientation associated with such canonical figures as John Locke, David Hume, William Blackstone, Adam Smith, Immanuel Kant, James Madison, Alexis de Tocqueville, and John Stuart Mill. Despite the many differences dividing the thinkers commonly placed under the liberal aegis, certain fixed points unite writers in this field of thought. As political theorist Judith Shklar asserts in her well-known essay "The Liberalism of Fear", "Liberalism has only one overriding aim: to secure the political conditions that are necessary for the exercise of political freedom."[5] Noting the high priority liberals place on limiting the coercive powers of government, political theorist Stephen Holmes contends that "the highest political values, from a liberal perspective, are psychological security and personal independence for all, legal impartiality within a single system of laws applied equally to all, the human diversity fostered by liberty, and collective self-rule through elected government and uncensored discussion."[6] It is vital to understand, however, that while the liberal ideal was born in opposition to tyranny and is characterized by an abiding suspicion of state power, liberals are not, as a rule, antistatist in orientation. Instead, recognizing that anarchy, too, poses a grave threat to individual liberty, liberals characteristically stake their claim on the precarious middle ground between the state of nature and the total state, figuring government simultaneously as a necessary guarantor of individual liberty and the source of liberty's most serious threat.

Despite the ill-favor into which the label "liberal" has fallen in contemporary popular political discourse, there is an important sense in which, as political theorist Richard Bellamy observes, "we are all liberals now." By this, Bellamy means to say that "all major groupings employ the liberal language of rights, freedom, and equality to express and legitimize their views and demonstrate corresponding general acceptance of liberal conceptions of democracy and the market."[7] Observations such as Bellamy's provide important clues to understanding why it is that big government persists as a focal point of U.S. politics, eclipsing other pressing political issues, most notably an ongoing crisis in self-government reflected in disappointing rates of voter turnout and notoriously low levels of civic engagement in the political process more broadly defined. After all, while it is the case that the U.S. government is doing more than it ever has before, at the same time the citizenry seems to be doing even less. The fact that the growing disconnect between the people and their government is reflexively and uncritically depicted as a problem of too much government, rather than too little public participation, highlights the dominance that liberalism—a philosophical ideal that prioritizes respect for individual rights over the importance of civic life—plays in determining the course and tenor of political discourse in the United States.

This book offers an in-depth analysis of the meaning of limited government in recent liberal political thought. Although the value of limited government is uniformly recognized in U.S. political discourse, just what limited government entails remains far from clear. Particularly in the wake of the emergence of the modern legislative state, Anglo-American liberal political philosophers since the mid-twentieth century have focused significant attention on the question "how much government is too much?" While liberals have long been centrally concerned with the problem of constraining governmental coercion, in the post-New Deal era this longstanding philosophical inquiry has taken on special urgency, as the reach of legislative power in both the United States and Western Europe has expanded in historically unprecedented ways. Responding to (and at times, fomenting) public concern about the dangers to individual liberty posed by the explosion of big government initiatives, liberal political philosophers writing in the latter part of the twentieth century dedicated themselves to finally resolving the question of where the limits of legislative power lie in a liberal democracy. However, by the end of the century, liberals found themselves locked in a stalemate, riven by a deep and seemingly unbridgeable divide between libertarians and welfarists.

The next two chapters offer a review of these debates, focusing on two of the twentieth century's most prominent liberal thinkers—F. A. Hayek and John Rawls. Although Hayek and Rawls typically are positioned as exemplars of the two major competing poles of opinion dividing liberals on the question of the legitimacy of the modern welfare state, my analysis emphasizes a neglected point of agreement—their shared recognition that the question of the scope and reach of government cannot be decisively resolved by philosophical fiat. Conceding, if often only implicitly, that the question of the acceptable extent of coercion must be left open for debate in the political process itself, Hayek and Rawls inadvertently lay the foundation for an alternative liberal conceptualization of limited government, one which shifts the emphasis from the identification of pre-political limiting principles to an understanding of the political processes out of which decisions concerning the appropriate use of state power emerge.

In the second half of the book, I advocate for a new direction in liberal theorizing about limited government for the twenty-first century, highlighting the central role that democratic politics, rather than philosophical principles, plays in determining the uses and limits of power in a liberal regime. Taking inspiration from recent works in the fields of democratic theory and cultural studies, the final two chapters probe contemporary popular political culture to gain a keener understanding of the democratic political process itself and the possibilities for limiting government. Offering in-depth discussions of examples from everyday life in the United States, including the reality TV craze and recent public furors over perceived threats to privacy rights, I consider the distinctive challenges facing liberals committed to maintaining meaningful limits on government in an increasingly complex world.

It is my hope that the arguments advanced in the following pages will not only contribute to ongoing philosophical inquiry into the question of the legitimate limits of official coercion in a liberal democracy, but that the discussion may also shed light on public debates by helping to clarify what a commitment to limited government does—and does not—demand as a matter of political practice.

Limited Government: From Legislative Supremacy to Line-Drawing

It is in a certain sense surprising that antigovernment sentiment runs so high in the United States, given that this is a nation which imagines itself to exemplify the principle of popular sovereignty. After all, one might expect the citizens of a country founded on the premise that government speaks in the name of "we the people" to be less rather than more suspicious of governmental power. The distinctively American ambivalence toward its government reveals a central aspect of the inheritance liberalism has bequeathed to U.S. political culture, as liberalism's investment in individual liberty places the liberal ideal in an intimate but uneasy relationship with the notion of democratic self-rule. Since its very inception, liberalism has had what might best be described as a love/hate relationship with democracy. On the one hand, liberals historically have recognized democratic self-rule to be the form of government most consistent with a core commitment to autonomy and self-determination, and for this reason, liberals long have distinguished themselves as strong proponents of equal voting rights, free speech, and other core democratic values. On the other hand, liberals also have been acutely sensitive to the dangers that majoritarian rule poses to the rights of individuals, particularly those in the minority. This abiding ambivalence about democracy is reflected in U.S. political culture, where Americans typically exalt the virtues of democracy even while disparaging the incompetence of their fellow citizens.[8]

For liberal philosophers, the ideal of limited government serves to mediate the fundamental tension between liberalism and democracy. Limited government stands for the idea of democracy enabled, but always contained. As I discuss in the subsequent two chapters, twentieth-century liberal theorists have regarded it as axiomatic that a fixed and firm boundary be drawn to distinguish the realm of public authority from the domain of private life, thereby curtailing the ability of democratically accountable legislatures to authorize incursions against individual liberties. In the words of political theorist Will Kymlicka, "Liberalism expresses its commitment to modern liberty *by sharply separating* the public power of the state from the private relationships of civil society, and *by setting strict limits* on the state's ability to intervene in private life" (emphasis added).[9] As exemplified in Kymlicka's description, liberal theorists typically portray the social world in terms of a division of spheres, zones, or realms, extolling the importance of "sharp separations," "strict limits," or what Isaiah Berlin famously refers to as the "frontier" beyond which public authority may never reach. Insisting on the need to "draw the line" and "fix the limit," liberals defend the public/private divide as the central axis along which to divide social geography. In the pages which follow, I refer to this way of conceptualizing limited government as the line-drawing approach. As I use the term here, line-drawing implies a notion of limited government in which the limits on government's coercive power are established pre-politically, outside of and above the play of politics, and safeguarded from revision or repeal by ordinary political actors. Typically, the idea of rights figure prominently in liberal discussions of limited government, marking the line beyond which government may not cross. Thus, a right to free speech implies that government may not pass laws limiting the exercise of speech, and a right to reproductive choice means that legislatures may not interfere with a woman's decision to seek an abortion. In this way, line-drawing implies the existence of explicit, specific constraints on content of laws, rather than a provision for checks on the exercise of legislative power imposed via formal or institutional constraints, such as a rule which says that all laws must be prospective in application, or a requirement that laws be authorized by both houses of a bicameral legislature. The close association between the discourse of line-drawing and the idea of specified rights points to the central role played by the idea of constitutional entrenchment and judicial review in line-drawing conceptions of limited government, where a constitution is conceived as a preserve of fundamental rights not subject to reconsideration in the everyday political process, and the judiciary, as the guardian of those rights, is figured as a body above the political fray.[10]

While the rhetoric characteristic of twentieth-century liberal thought implies the necessity of line-drawing, liberals have not always approached the problem of limited government in this manner. I turn now to a brief exploration of the origins of liberal thinking about limited government, tracing the ideal back to the writings of John Locke, the great seventeenth-century English philosopher often referred to as the founder of the modern liberalism. Interestingly, Locke's conception of limited government differs in fundamental ways from the line-drawing approach more familiar in twentieth-century discussions of limited government. Locke's views are most extensively detailed in his *Second Treatise on Government*, published on the heels of the Glorious Revolution of 1688. In the *Second Treatise*, Locke offers a version of natural law theory with a radical twist, defending the principle of popular sovereignty as the legitimate basis for civil society. However, as political theorist Jeremy Waldron observes, Locke's ideas about limited government as presented in the *Second Treatise* suggest a puzzle, for "Locke is supposed to be the founder of liberal constitutionalism, the theorist of natural rights, the philosopher of the limited legislature. So why in the *Second Treatise* does he argue that the legislature is supreme, that it must never be subject to any other body, and thus to judicial review or anything else, at least while the government lasts?"[11] As Waldron points out, in the *Second Treatise* Locke defends the principle of legislative supremacy—an institutional arrangement which implies no provision for a written constitution, judicial review, or an executive veto of legislation. Instead, Locke figures the legislature as the branch of government designed to be representative of and accountable to the people, who are understood collectively as the highest political authority.

From a contemporary standpoint, an endorsement of legislative supremacy such as that found in Locke's writings implies nothing less than a renunciation of the commitment to limited government, for a supreme legislature would seem to be one whose ability to authorize coercion is, by definition, unconstrained. But, as Waldron explains, Locke was convinced that a supreme legislature could also be a limited one. To understand his logic, it is useful to begin with a consideration of the role that natural law theory plays in his ideal regime. According to Locke, legislators are bound, in the first instance, to obey the precepts of natural law. Locke explains:

> The Law of Nature stands as an Eternal Rule to all Men, Legislators as well as others. The rules that they make for other Mens Actions, must, as well as their own and other Mens Actions, be conformable to the Law of Nature, i.e. to the Will of God, of which that is a Declaration, and the fundamental Law of Nature being the preservation of mankind, no Human Sanction can be good, or valid against it.[12]

As Waldron points out, here a serious challenge rises to the fore: even if all of the members of a legislature agree that natural law establishes constraints on legislative power, it seems inevitable that disagreement will arise about just what it is natural law prescribes when it comes to specific questions of legislation. Does natural law require respect for reproductive rights or a governmental ban on abortions? Does natural law support or reject same-sex marriage? And what could natural law possibly have to tell us about questions such as whether tax rates should be based on a progressive or a flat scale?

Crucially, in the Lockean regime the task of giving content to natural law falls to the legislature itself.[13] As the body charged with representing the people in all of their diversity, and as a body whose members are bound to obey any law they see fit to propagate, the legislature is, in Locke's view, the institution best positioned to resolve problems rooted in the irreducible indeterminacy of natural law. Significantly, Locke sees no conflict of interest arising from the fact that the legislature is assigned the task of deliberating about the nature of its own limits—a view which seems dangerously naïve when judged from a contemporary standpoint. Who among us would be willing to trust that legislative power could be constrained simply by relying on legislators' own commitment to respect the dictates of natural law? In contrast to modern cynicism about the good intentions of politicians, however, Locke's plan for limited government rests on the belief that moral and cultural limits are sufficient as constraints on legislatures, and that provision for more rigorous institutional limits are unnecessary.[14] For Locke, the emphasis rests on cultivating in the citizenry at large a proper respect for the value of natural rights, a respect Locke believes is sufficient to steer liberal subjects in monitoring and guiding their representatives, and to discourage legislators from propagating laws which conflict with broadly held civic values.

Locke's ideas about good government were among the first British imports brought to the shores of what would eventually become the United States. Chief among the ideas the seventeenth-century colonists took with them was the idea that legislative supremacy is the principle of government best suited to a people committed to popular sovereignty. Rebelling against their brethren back home, the American colonists saw themselves as the true champions of the noble principles for which the Glorious Revolution had been fought. Indicting the British Parliament for turning its back on the principle of popular sovereignty, the colonists hoped to redeem the corrupted ideal of self-rule. In this spirit, local governments in the burgeoning colonies were organized around what political theorist Isaac Kramnick describes as a prescription for nothing less than "the absolute dominance of the legislature" within each of the states.[15] Strikingly, provision for electoral accountability was almost the only safeguard offered against the risk of legislative excess, as no serious attempt was made to balance powers in the early years of colonial governance. Instead, state constitutions allowed only for virtually powerless governors to head the executive branch, while the judicial branch was made dependent on the legislature for decisions regarding appointments, terms of service, and salaries, as well as for decisions regarding the final review of cases.[16] And although state constitutions did include bills of rights imposing strict constraints on executive power, it was widely understood that these rights were not meant to limit the power of the legislatures, but rather, in the words of historian Jack Rakove, "to *guide* [the legislature] in exercising its discretionary authority rather than to *restrain* legislative power by creating an armory of judicially enforceable rights."[17]

In time, enthusiasm for legislative supremacy waned among the colonists. State legislatures during the period governed by the first national constitution, the *Articles of Confederation*, progressively alienated several key segments of the population. Historian Gordon Wood suggests that the end of the era of sovereign state legislatures was finally brought about not by elites angling for the augmentation of federal power, but rather by "the repeated and intensifying denials by various groups that the state legislatures adequately spoke for the people."[18] While Wood stresses the idea of a revolution from "below," then, Kramnick highlights the significance as well of the opposition of the well-off minority threatened by the "redistributive nature of so much of the legislation coming out of the state legislatures." Kramnick explains that "the concern of many who repudiated the Articles . . . would be not simply the immense power of state legislatures, abstractly considered, but the substantive content of the legislation passed by these all powerful legislatures as it threatened vested economic interests and private rights."[19] But even as complaints about legislative excess multiplied, would-be reformers struggled to gather momentum for change. With memories of the indignities suffered under British rule still vivid and the revolutionary spirit still strong, any proposal to shift power away from the people was sure to encounter resistance, even in the face of widespread disappointment with the actual experience of democratic self-government.

In facing the failure of legislative supremacy as a self-regulating system of governance, the aspiring founders of the United States found themselves confronting head-on a constitutive ambivalence at the very center of the young republic's self-understanding. The ambivalence concerned popular sovereignty, which the revolutionaries regarded as both their greatest accomplishment and their most serious liability. Then (as now) the ideal of rule by the people was exalted even as the lived experience of popular sovereignty was disparaged. In such a climate, the case for reform had to be broached with delicacy and discretion. Proponents of a new constitution would ultimately settle on a strategy which would demand an extraordinary feat of rhetorical finesse, taxing the skills even of the consummately gifted cohort of politician-philosophers known to us now as the framers of the U.S. Constitution. For how would it be possible to make convincing the decidedly counter-intuitive case that the campaign to limit the "people's legislatures" was being waged in the name of popular sovereignty itself?[20]

When the ratification debates began in earnest in the fall of 1787, the task of defending the seemingly contradictory plan for a stronger yet more limited government fell largely to James Madison. While affirming the principle of popular sovereignty, Madison sought to uproot the standing assumption of a necessary relationship between the principle of popular sovereignty and rule by popular legislatures. Based on recent experience, Madison proclaimed it to be undeniably the case that "the instability, injustice, and confusion introduced into the public councils have, in truth, been the mortal diseases under which popular governments have everywhere perished."[21] While acknowledging that the people "seem never for a moment to have turned their eyes from the danger, to liberty, from the overgrown and all-grasping prerogative of an hereditary magistrate, supported and fortified by an hereditary branch of the legislative authority," Madison notes with dismay that "[t]hey seem never to have recollected the danger from legislative usurpations, which, by assembling all power in the same hands, must lead to the same tyranny as is threatened by executive usurpations."[22] Regrettably but undeniably, the colonists discovered that rights were as insecure in a regime ruled by popular legislatures as they had been under monarchical rule. Legislative supremacy offered not protection from tyranny, but only an alternative route to it. The question, then, was how to bring the legislatures back into line. While it was evident that the legislatures needed to be checked, it was not so clear at the outset how this would be accomplished. In this regard it is worth noting that while we think of the U.S. Constitution as virtually synonymous with the Bill of Rights, the original constitutional

proposal supported by Madison did not even include these critical amendments. Instead, Madison and others preferred a plan to constrain legislative power dynamically, through an intricately designed system of checks
and balances. Throughout most of the constitutional convention, Madison
ardently resisted the effort to include a Bill of Rights, dismissing the
amendments as mere "parchment barriers," offering only a hollow promise of protection. In the end, however, advocates for the amendments
prevailed, with popular sentiment clearly aligned with those like Thomas
Jefferson, who, while agreeing that the Bill of Rights might fall short of
a perfect guarantee, nonetheless prevailed in his insistence that "half a loaf
is better than no bread."[23]

Though it was not so clear at the time, victory for proponents of the
Bill of Rights was critical in laying the groundwork for a fundamental
shift in the way limited government was conceived in the United States,
from a view rooted in the principle of legislative supremacy to the more
familiar line-drawing approach discussed earlier. The shift first began to
crystallize some fifteen years after the founding, when the great U.S.
Supreme Court Justice John Marshall handed down his decision in the
landmark 1803 case *Marbury v. Madison*.[24] The *Marbury* case arose from a
seemingly trivial dispute concerning the contested appointment of a
low-level government functionary, William Marbury, as a justice of the
peace in the District of Columbia. As one of outgoing-President John
Adams's "midnight appointments," Marbury's appointment was authorized
as part of a last-minute effort to stack the judicial branch with personnel
sympathetic to the position of his ousted Federalist Party administration.
In the haste, Marbury's commission was signed, sealed, but never delivered
to the appropriate office. The question was whether the new administration
was legally bound to honor Marbury's commission. Moving far beyond
the apparent scope of the dispute, Justice Marshall frames the case as
one which raises fundamental questions about the allocation of public
authority between the legislative and judicial branches. Declaring that
"the Constitution sets limits on government and that those limits may
not be mistaken, or forgotten, the Constitution is written," Marshall goes
on to insist that the Constitution is "the fundamental and paramount law

of the nation," and that "it is emphatically the province and the duty of the judicial department to say what the law is." But why should this power rest in the hands of an unelected panel of legal elites, rather than fall to the democratically elected legislators explicitly charged with representing the will of the people? Marshall summarily dismisses the idea that legislatures rather than courts should have final interpretive say over constitutional text as simply too absurd to warrant serious engagement. In a few cursory paragraphs, he briskly rehearses the case against legislative supremacy, charging that it would "subvert the very foundation of all written constitutions" by granting "to the legislature a practical and real omnipotence, with the same breath which professes to restrict their powers within narrow limits." Instead, Marshall concludes that acceptance of a written constitution no less than entails the principle of judicial supremacy.

Marshall's argument in *Marbury* represents a very different way of thinking about limited government than the position espoused by Locke some one hundred years earlier, and each of these two approaches to limited government has distinctive strengths and weaknesses. As I discussed in the context of Locke's scheme, legislative supremacy relies in the last instance on faith in the good will of the very legislators whose power liberals believe it is so important to contain. In light of this concern, perhaps it is not surprising that today we find a logic more akin to Marshall's undergirding the rhetoric adopted by liberals concerned with limited government. But while line-drawing may have prevailed as liberalism's dominant approach, it too is problematic. Among the most serious challenges facing advocates of line-drawing is the charge that in seeking to limit legislative authority, line-drawing undermines democracy. This concern has been voiced most often in the context of a critique of judicial review, an institutional arrangement which figures judges as the ultimate guardians of individual rights whose primary task is to check democracy's excesses. While commitment to judicial review remains strong among liberal democratic theorists, many have nonetheless expressed concern about the seemingly ineliminable tension between the ideals of liberal constitutionalism and democracy.[25] In the words of legal theorist Sotirios Barber, "[t]he problem that dominates American constitutional theory in the twentieth century is that of reconciling the power of an electorally unaccountable judiciary with norms of democratic responsibility."[26] Why, in a regime which prides itself on rule by the people, should we tolerate judicial review of majoritarian decisions? Dogged by what Alexander Bickel famously dubbed the "countermajoritarian difficulty," liberal legal theorists have struggled with the problem of how to justify higher-law constraints in a regime based on the principle of popular sovereignty. Bellamy offers this pointed description of the dilemma:

> On the one hand, the justification for democratic procedures most commonly rests on liberal assumptions. Standard liberal arguments for democracy range from the importance of consent due to the moral primacy of the individual, to the role of critical argument and the diversity of opinion for the discovery of truth. On the other hand, liberal institutional arrangements, such as the separation of powers and the role of law, have frequently been interpreted as constraints upon democracy, albeit necessary ones if democracy is not to undermine itself. The paradox arises from the fact that liberalism provides a philosophical basis for regarding democracy as the only valid source of law whilst apparently appealing to some higher law in order to limit democracy itself.[27]

Opting for line-drawing over legislative supremacy, twentieth-century liberals may be said to prefer the discomfort of the countermajoritarian dilemma to the alternative, which we might call the *majoritarian* dilemma— the threat to liberty posed by a legislature figured both as the source and subject of limits. But what if, instead of worrying about how to justify constraints on the democratic process, liberals were to embrace the Lockean-inspired notion that in a liberal society, there can be no higher authority than the voice of the people, a conclusion that, at least some would say, flows necessarily from liberalism's core commitment to the principles of individual liberty and self-determination. While the countermajoritarian difficulty makes liberals uncomfortable, the alternative— confronting the majoritarian difficulty—is downright terrifying, for at least from the contemporary perspective, it seems tantamount to a concession of the impossibility of limited government. Thus, although line-drawing as a strategy for limiting government exists in uneasy tension with the competing value of popular sovereignty, liberal thinkers generally cling to this strategy out of fear of something even worse.

Liberalism Confronts the Welfare State

For twentieth-century Anglo-American liberal philosophers, the introduction of the New Deal in the United States is the signal event, standing as the often implicit reference point for ongoing discussions of limited government. Although the purview of the U.S. government has expanded uninterruptedly since its inception, the New Deal era is widely regarded as nothing short of a revolution, inaugurating an unprecedented era of governmental involvement in the everyday lives of every citizen. In the decades since the New Deal initiatives were first introduced, American politics has been deeply riven by debates about the role government should play in everyday life. In this climate, liberal thinkers' longstanding inquiry into the meaning of limited government has been transformed from a philosophical inquiry into a debate with immediate and obvious political relevance. In an effort to finally settle the debate about how much government is too much, twentieth-century liberal theorists embarked on a quest for consensus regarding liberalism's first principles, with the hope that agreement on core values might provide a standard against which the legitimacy of specific policies could be assessed.

In the wake of significant soul-searching, two main camps of opinion among liberals emerged in the latter part of the twentieth century concerning the nature of fundamental rights and, by implication, the limits of government. Most prominent in the theoretical literature have been the voices of those theorists who contend that a liberal government can and should play a significant role in maintaining the underlying social and economic conditions necessary for individuals to enjoy their liberties. These thinkers, often referred to as redistributionists or welfarist liberals, defend a conception of individual liberty which entails certain positive obligations on the part of the liberal state. On the other side of the debate are self-proclaimed "classical liberals," often referred to as libertarians, who argue instead that a proper respect for liberty can be maintained only with the most minimal intervention by the state in individual lives. For thinkers on this side of the divide, a liberal government must adopt a laissez-faire approach to the economy and to the regulation of social life, limiting interventions to a few circumscribed tasks, usually considered to be those having to do with law-and-order and national security.

The next two chapters offer an in-depth consideration of these contrasting perspectives, focusing on the writings of F. A. Hayek and John Rawls, exemplars, respectively, of the two competing camps of opinion within liberalism—libertarianism and welfarism. Rawls is widely considered the most important liberal thinker of the twentieth century, one who accomplished the rare feat of being recognized as a canonical figure in his own time. In 1971, Rawls, a member of the Philosophy Department at Harvard, published his instant classic *A Theory of Justice*, a work that has spawned a vast critical literature in the field of political theory and beyond. In this book, Rawls presents a comprehensive reworking of the liberal ideal, seeking to finally end the longstanding association between the free market and the minimal state to defend the claim, among others, that the redistribution of wealth may advance, rather than offend, the cause of individual liberty. Although Rawls won the hearts and minds of the vast majority of liberal academics, it is Hayek who has achieved far greater popular acclaim across the United States, Great Britain, and in the formerly communist eastern bloc countries of Europe as well.[28] Born in 1899, Hayek was deeply influenced by many of the thinkers associated with the Austrian School of Economics. Upon completing a course of study with Ludwig Von Mises in Vienna, Hayek left continental Europe for England in 1931 and spent the next two decades writing and teaching at the London School of Economics. Hayek's major claim to fame is his publication in 1945 of *The Road to Serfdom*. In this slim but incendiary volume, Hayek memorably warned in the most dire of terms that it would only be a matter of time before the apparently benevolent welfare state devolved into a tyrannous "total state." A tireless scholar, Hayek went on to publish in an array of fields, including economics, law, philosophy, and social theory, producing scholarly works until well beyond his eightieth year.

Although there are other prominent theorists who might have been considered for this study, there are special advantages to staging a comparison between these two in particular. Rawls is widely recognized to be the consummate liberal theorist of the twentieth-century welfare state, earning this status on the basis of a meticulously elaborated defense of the welfarist implications of liberalism. Though there are other interesting and important liberals of a kindred orientation, it is Rawls's account that continues to serve as the focal point of critical attention from scholars. In selecting a representative of the classical liberal wing of the tradition, one draws from a much narrower field. Although libertarianism has flourished in the United States since the New Deal as a popular movement, the perspective has long struggled for philosophical bearings. Arguably the most well-respected and intellectually formidable libertarian philosopher to emerge in the last half century is Robert Nozick, but in his later writing Nozick himself recanted central aspects of the argument he originally presented as a defense of ideal.[29] Amongst those libertarians who remain—including Milton Friedman, Murray Rothbard, and Tyler Machan—Hayek stands out as the most intellectually rigorous and complex thinker among them.[30]

In addition to being exemplary theorists' of their respective positions, there is an additional reason I have chosen to focus on Hayek and Rawls. As I discuss in chapter three, upon reading Rawls's *A Theory of Justice*, Hayek wrote approvingly that he had "no basic quarrel" with the argument presented in the book.[31] Given the widely held image of Rawls and Hayek as representatives of warring liberal camps, Hayek's pronouncement is shocking. In presenting a comparative analysis of Hayek and Rawls, I hope to help make sense of Hayek's surprising declaration by drawing attention to a crucial similarity uniting these two thinkers—the fact that neither lives up to his reputation as a stalwart advocate for his respective position on the legitimacy of the modern welfare state. Despite the uncompromising rhetoric adopted by each, neither ends up taking a firm stand on the specific question of where to draw the line between public power and private rights; indeed, both provide visions of the liberal ideal that are striking in their vagueness. In the case of both Hayek and Rawls, I root the resistance to line-drawing in a commitment even more fundamental than an interest in limited government—a commitment to honor the principle of neutrality. As political philosopher Charles Larmore explains, modern liberalism is based on the conviction that, as a matter of social fact, "reasonable people tend naturally to differ and disagree about the nature of the good life."[32] For liberals, the term neutrality does not imply an attitude of indifference regarding moral and political questions, but rather, a recognition that reasonable people may disagree about issues of fundamental importance in a liberal society, including what the meaning of justice is, which rights individuals should be accorded, and what kinds of services the government is obliged to provide. Larmore characterizes the essence of liberalism as rooted in "the hope that, despite this tendency toward disagreement about matters of ultimate significance, we can find some way of living together that avoids the rule of force."[33] What this requires, from a liberal point of view, is a society grounded in the identification of neutral principles, "those we can justify without assuming the validity of those views of the good on which people reasonably disagree."[34]

Recognition of the fact of reasonable disagreement creates a paradox for liberals committed to limited government—when limited government is taken to imply pre-political line-drawing. While the purpose of limiting government is to insure that official coercion is not used to enforce controversial notions about the good life, decisions about where the limits of government lie inevitably rest on contested ideas about rights and justice. Unless truly neutral principles of justice can be identified, however, limited government becomes a sham—a way of enforcing a controversial theory of rights under the pretense of limiting the ability of legislatures to violate rights. And although liberals as different as Hayek and Rawls recognize the challenge that a commitment to neutrality poses for those seeking to draw lines limiting legislative power, the rhetoric of line-drawing pervades their writing and that of many commentators.

Reading twentieth-century liberal theorizing against the grain, I contend that Hayek and Rawls are united in a refusal to presettle the limits of legislative power. While Hayek is commonly portrayed as a hard-core libertarian, in chapter one I make the case that his bark is worse than his bite: while he sharply criticizes redistributionist social policies, he ultimately concedes that liberalism affords no principled basis for prohibiting them. To the end, Hayek steadfastly refuses to issue categorical bans against "big government" initiatives, instead allowing for the possibility that legislators in his ideal liberal regime will pass laws he considers foolish and even dangerous. In the case of Rawls, critics accuse him of trivializing the democratic process by advocating the establishment of pre-political principles of justice whose very purpose it is to preempt political debate about fundamental questions of justice. However, in chapter two I show that there is much more room for debate and disagreement in Rawls's ideal regime than his own rhetoric implies. Despite important differences, then, I conclude that much less divides Hayek and Rawls when it comes to theorizing limited government than is generally supposed. In both accounts, liberal principles are defined in such a way as to leave crucial questions about the scope and reach of government open to resolution in the everyday political process. Instead of guarantees, whether of welfare rights or individual rights, both theorists allow legislators to authorize a wide range of governmental interventions, unfettered by any but the most minimal constraints. Unfortunately, this restraint with respect to propounding limits has been obscured by commentators who have tended to exaggerate the positionality of both Hayek and Rawls. Thus, Hayek generally has been dismissed by political theorists as a libertarian extremist unworthy of serious consideration. And while Rawls enjoys significantly more respect amongst academic commentators than does Hayek, he too has been subject to attack in a vast, critical literature dedicated to proving that his project fails to live up to the presumed goal of demonstrating that liberalism entails a commitment to a robust welfare state.

Rethinking the Liberal Theory of Limited Government

Despite the predominance of the rhetoric of line-drawing in liberal accounts of limited government, it turns out that liberals' commitment to respect the fact of reasonable disagreement precludes the possibility of pre-determining the content of fundamental principles of justice. Does the impossibility of line-drawing mean that liberals must abandon the goal of limited government? Not necessarily. In the early years of the new millennium, theorists sympathetic to the liberal project have begun to explore alternative approaches to limiting government, strategies which are premised on a recognition that in a liberal democracy, fundamental questions about the meaning of justice must be left for determination in the political process itself. In seeking to move beyond the line-drawing model of limited government, these thinkers place greater emphasis on the importance of institutional reforms designed to produce collective decisions from within the political process itself which will honor the diversity of opinion characteristic of a liberal society.

In chapter four, I present a study of the recent writings of political and legal philosopher Jeremy Waldron, one of the leading voices in the effort to shift the emphasis in liberal theorizing on limited government from a debate about pre-political limiting principles toward a focus on the political process as the site for making determinations about the appropriate uses and limits of political power. Waldron conceives of a limited government as one in which the legislature conforms to fundamental principles of justice which are themselves the outcome of a political deliberation. His is a vision of limited government which emphasizes the need for democratic control of government, rather than philosophical control of democracy. Specifically, Waldron defends "the dignity of legislation" as a counter to what he believes is a longstanding prejudice in liberal theory against legislative politics and in favor of judicial supremacy. While there is much to commend in Waldron's approach, however, in this chapter I argue that Waldron does not go far enough in rethinking liberalism's view of limited government. Implicitly endorsing what I call "the ideology of separated powers," Waldron uncritically accepts the notion of the judiciary as a sphere of elites and the legislature as the people's branch. This exaggerated view of the distinction between the branches leads him to rest his faith on an idealized portrait of legislative politics, while neglecting the need to politicize power more broadly in a liberal regime.

The limitations of Waldron's account suggest that liberals who seek to move beyond line-drawing must embark on a much more sustained inquiry into the nature and practice of democratic politics as a crucial first step toward the development of a viable model of limited government, one which rests on a recognition of both the capacities as well as the limits of democratic decision making. If fundamental decisions about the scope and reach of political power are to be made in the political process itself, then more attention is due to the quality of that process. For this reason, in the last two chapters of the book the argument takes a very different course, shifting from a focus on philosophical debates to a wider-ranging consideration of popular political culture. In doing so, the concluding chapters are meant to underscore my suggestion that liberal theorists attend more closely to questions about the practice of democratic politics. Taking political culture, rather than philosophical texts, as my object of inquiry, the final two chapters exemplify the kind of methodological shift I urge liberals to undertake, widening their lens of inquiry and undertaking a more thorough investigation into the complexities of democracy.

Chapter five presents an inquiry into the possibilities and limits of political participation in a liberal democratic regime, focusing on the institution of voting in particular. The discussion revolves around an unlikely topic—reality TV—both as a way to generate insights about the social meaning of the vote, as well as to consider alternate modes of institutionalizing it. This chapter's exploration of some of the hidden complexities of voting in a liberal democratic context suggests that in recognizing the significance of the legislative process in a liberal regime, liberals must also take a more active role in re-thinking the kinds of political processes and practices likely to generate legislative outcomes consistent with an underlying commitment to honoring pluralism while respecting individual rights. Examples of voting on reality TV reveal some of the inherent limits of voting as a mode of political participation, limits that should give liberals committed to limited government pause.

Finally, in chapter six I offer some concluding reflections on the ongoing value and significance of the ideal of privacy, a concept which lies at the very heart of the line-drawing approach to limited government. In moving beyond the line-drawing model of limited government, one must ask whether liberals should continue to speak of social space as if it can be neatly divided along the public/private axis. This chapter urges liberals to rethink the centrality of the public/private distinction by suggesting that the history of governmental enforcement of privacy doctrine in the United States illustrates the limits of line-drawing, and more broadly, that transformations in U.S. social life pose serious challenges to the enduring coherence of the public/private distinction. However, while giving up on the public/private distinction means giving up on the promise of fixed guarantees, it does not mean abandoning the goal of containing power. Instead of vesting faith in pre-given limits, I argue that the urgent task facing liberal theorists today is to lend a critical voice to efforts to enlarge and enliven the practice of democratic politics.

In offering a critical assessment of recent developments in the way liberals conceptualize limited government, I hope that the discussion presented in the following pages will be useful to both scholarly and popular audiences in clarifying what limited government means in a liberal society. And in seeking to chart a course for future theorizing about limited government in the twenty-first century, I hope the conversation will spur further efforts to rethink a problem which lies at the very heart of the liberal democratic ideal.

CHAPTER TWO

Liberalism Confronts the Welfare State

Since the mid-twentieth century, Anglo-American liberal political philosophy has been dominated by controversy over the question how much government is too much. Spurred by the growth of the welfare state apparatus in the Anglo-American world, liberal political theorists have been entangled in fierce debates over where to draw the line between public power and private rights. Liberal thinkers have always been centrally concerned with delimiting the appropriate scope and reach of legislative power, but in recent decades liberalism's longstanding philosophical inquiry has assumed a degree of political urgency as the regulatory and redistributive capacities of the federal government in the United States in particular have expanded in historically unprecedented ways, propelled by forces ranging from the social to the technological.[1] Responding to the emergence of the modern welfare state, some liberal thinkers have advocated for a position its proponents describe as a return to "classical liberalism," so-called because of the emphasis placed on protecting individual property rights through the imposition of strict limits on the ability of the government to implement redistributionist public policies. For thinkers in this camp—commonly referred to as libertarians[2]—it is agreed that a liberal government should adopt a laissez-faire posture toward the regulation of the economy and other aspects of social and personal life, limiting interventions to a few circumscribed tasks, generally those having to do with maintaining law-and-order and protecting national security.

F. A. Hayek is known as one of the twentieth century's most tireless exponents of the libertarian position, and in this chapter I explore his distinctive contribution to liberal thinking about limited government. Born in Austria in 1899, Hayek's intellectual trajectory was established early in life, while he was still a student at the University of Vienna.[3] It was there that Hayek first encountered the theories associated with the Austrian School of Economics, a brand of economic thought with origins in the writings of economist Carl Menger and which has come to be associated with antisocialist, anti-collectivist, and pro-liberal capitalist politics. Following a brief stint as a civil servant upon the completion of his studies, Hayek left Austria for England in 1931, and spent the next two decades at the London School of Economics (LSE). At the LSE, Hayek solidified his reputation as one of the leading economic theorists of the day, gaining notoriety for publicly sparring with his Cambridge colleague economist John Keynes.[4] In 1945, Hayek published the work for which he would always be best known, *The Road to Serfdom*. In that now (in)famous volume, Hayek declares war on what he labels the "planned economy," taking aim at state-sponsored "social justice" policies which rely on the coercive powers of the state to engineer the good society. *The Road to Serfdom* launched Hayek's career as a public intellectual and cemented his place in the pantheon of libertarian heroes, but it also undermined his reputation as a serious academic in the eyes of many established scholars.[5] After World War II, Hayek moved to the Committee on Social Thought at the University of Chicago (after been denied a position in the Department of Economics.) In 1961, he published *The Constitution of Liberty*, the book which would stand as his most substantial and ambitious work of liberal philosophy. Hayek remained professionally active until well into his 80th year, publishing throughout the 1970s the three volume *Law, Legislation, and Liberty* series in which he presents a detailed vision of his ideal liberal society. When he died in 1992, Hayek left behind a lasting legacy of scholarly writing in an array of fields, including economics, law, philosophy, and social theory.

Despite winning the Nobel Prize in economic sciences in 1974 and garnering a host of other academic accolades throughout his academic career, Hayek generally is treated as a minor figure in the annals of twentieth-century liberal thought, dwarfed in stature by such thinkers as Isaiah Berlin and John Rawls. Frequently ignored in political theory survey courses, and marginalized in the contemporary critical literature on liberalism, Hayek typically is portrayed as little more than a cold war crank—that is, when he is given consideration at all. Perceived more as an ideologue than a serious thinker, contemporary liberal theorists have been quick to dismiss Hayek as a "laissez-faire extremist,"[6] one of the "zealots of laissez-faire liberalism,"[7] and even an "anti-egalitarian."[8] Political theorist Stephen Holmes reflects the consensus view in depicting Hayek as a hard-core minimalist, one who, in Holmes' words, believes that "liberalism is *wholly incompatible* with positive programs of public provision, all of which require confiscatory taxation" (emphasis added).[9] Depictions such as these reinforce the widely held impression—which I challenge—that Hayek defends a strict principle of non-intervention, and that he opposes in all cases a wide range of familiar welfare state policies.

Among those few political theorists who have seriously grappled with Hayek's thought, most have been highly critical of his approach to limiting government, the ambition which lies at the heart of his vision of the ideal liberal society. In the scholarly literature surrounding Rawls's political writings, three main lines of attack predominate. The first is the charge that in presenting a liberal vision of limited government, Hayek draws the line between public power and private rights in the wrong place, adopting a far too narrow view of the role legislatures should play in ordering public life.[10] From this perspective, Hayek's fundamental mistake is thought to lie in his contention that a commitment to individual liberty entails a defense of the minimal state. To the contrary say some proponents of the welfare state: fidelity to the liberal principle of individual liberty may even require government to enact redistributive social justice policies to counteract the inegalitarian forces of the free market, which tend to undermine individual liberty by depriving disadvantaged members of society of the ability to exercise the liberties liberals promote in the first place. The second line of attack against Hayek focuses not on the question of whether liberals should rally around the libertarian position, but rather on Hayek's failure to live up to his own promise to present a plan capable of constraining coercion.[11] This critique, which might be characterized as an internal rather than an external one, rests on the claim that Hayek fails on his own terms since his plan for limited government does not in the end guarantee that governmental coercion will stay within the narrow bounds insisted upon by classical liberals. Finally, a third line of critical inquiry revolves around the contention that Hayek's theory of limited government bespeaks an underlying contempt for democratic self-governance, and that the scheme he proposes for limited government does not merely "dethrone" but in fact dismantles democracy, replacing it with an elitist form of authoritarian rule.[12]

In the following discussion, I contend that these charges rest on pervasive misunderstandings about the nature of Hayek's approach to limiting government. Although Hayek is commonly portrayed as a libertarian fundamentalist, throughout his career he adopted a far more nuanced and far less severe position than most commentators recognize. Indeed, if Hayek was dogmatic about anything, it was his dislike of dogmatism itself—libertarian or otherwise. Crucially, Hayek steadfastly refused to advocate for categorical bans against welfarist and redistributionist initiatives, for, in his view, liberal principles neither demand nor foreclose laissez-faire economic policies. While there can be no question that Hayek was a strong opponent of welfarist public policies, he did not rest his opposition to the welfare state on a commitment to liberal principles alone. Rather, Hayek rooted his resistance to welfare state policies in a practical assessment of the consequences of adopting such policies. While invoking the absolutist rhetoric of line-drawing and issuing dire warnings about the dangers of even setting foot down the road to serfdom, behind the tough talk one finds in Hayek's works an approach to the problem of constraining coercion which implicitly acknowledges just how wide a field liberals must leave for legislative discretion. Too often, however, commentators simply have assumed that in his philosophical writings Hayek single-mindedly seeks to justify his libertarian policy preferences, and thus the critics have proceeded to condemn him both for embracing this goal and for failing to live up to it. But Hayek does no such thing, conceding that liberal principles themselves entail little by way of constraints on the scope of legislative discretion. While he sharply criticizes redistributionist social policies on the grounds of efficiency, Hayek ultimately acknowledges that there is no philosophical basis for prohibiting such legislation. The critics largely have misplaced their energies, then, in focusing on whether he draws the line between public power and private rights in the correct place. Relatedly, they have mistaken his criticism of democracy for an effort to dismantle democracy altogether, failing to appreciate the role that democratic politics plays in his portrait of the ideal liberal regime.

The portrait of Hayek that emerges in this chapter is an unconventional one, challenging the established reputation of Hayek as categorically opposed to welfarist public policies. Interestingly, one of the few critics to appreciate the degree the openness afforded to the legislature in Hayek's ideal liberal regime is one of his more unlikely admirers, Michel Foucault.[13] Near the end of his life, Foucault became increasingly curious about the classical liberal tradition. In a series of lectures delivered in the late 1970s, Foucault presented a study of "governmentality" which included a consideration of the way in which liberal thinking has come to define the terms and priorities of modern power relations.[14] In appraising these lectures, one commentator sympathetic to Foucault's radical views has observed—with more than a hint of scandal—that his "accounts of the anarcho-liberal thinkers indeed often evince a sense of (albeit value-neutral) intellectual attraction and esteem."[15] Contrary to those who might expect Hayek to defend strictly delineated, tightly enforced limits on the exercise of legislative power, in the following pages I suggest that Hayek's approach to limited government resonates with Foucault's insistence that "the liberty of men is never assured by the institutions and laws that are intended to guarantee them. . . . I think it can never be inherent in the structure of things to guarantee the exercise of freedom. The guarantee of freedom is freedom."[16] Although Hayek thinks it worthwhile to consider the form of laws and the design of institutions most likely to produce and support individual freedom, in the last instance he recognizes freedom in a liberal society to depend on collective choices, and to not be established by fixed guarantees.

As one final preliminary note, let me emphasize that in suggesting Hayek has been miscast as a libertarian dogmatist, the intent of the following discussion is not to redeem him in the eyes of the mainstream academy. Instead, I aim at the broader goal of helping to clarify where liberal theorists stand on the question of limited government in the wake of the emergence of the modern welfare state. Twentieth-century liberal political thought begins as the story of a search for foundational principles which might allow for a decisive resolution to long-raging debates over just how much government is too much. In the end, this quest for philosophical resolution leads Hayek to the conclusion that liberal principles do not in and of themselves contain answers to the most basic political, social, and economic questions of our time. Instead, Hayek finds that in charting a course for a liberal society, direction must come from within the political process itself.

Limited Government in the Hayekian Regime

Throughout his career, Hayek focused his critical energies on the threat to liberty posed by welfare state initiatives. Prone to alarmist rhetoric, Hayek's writings are peppered with uncompromising condemnations of the socialist project—an umbrella term he uses to include such familiar practices as redistributive taxation and social justice policies like unemployment insurance or public housing. In *The Road to Serfdom* (1944), Hayek bemoans the fact that "few are ready to recognize that the rise of fascism and Nazism was not a reaction against the socialist trends of the preceding period, but a necessary outcome of those tendencies."[17] In *The Constitution of Liberty* (1960) he avers that the welfare state "is bound to lead back to socialism and its coercive and essentially arbitrary methods."[18] In *The Mirage of Social Justice* (1976) Hayek opines that "the prevailing belief in 'social justice' is at present probably the gravest threat to most other values of a free civilization."[19] And in *The Political Order of a Free People* (1979) he reiterates his contention that " . . . socialism as much as fascism or communism inevitably leads into the totalitarian state and the destruction of the democratic order. . . . "[20] Hayek defines socialism broadly, as "the nationalization of the 'means of production, distribution, and exchange,' so that all economic activity might be directed according to a comprehensive plan toward some ideal of social justice."[21] The modern welfare state is premised, in Hayek's view, on "the desire to use the powers of government to insure a more even or more just distribution of goods."[22] From his standpoint, welfare state policies in arenas such as housing, health care, the regulation of food and drugs, and education, all reflect an underlying ambition to reengineer society in the image of a particular ideal of justice. Recognizing that there are many competing views of what social justice demands in terms of redistribution, Hayek nonetheless contends that all social justice programs rest on the shared premise that a just society can be produced through central planning, rather than trusting the spontaneous and undirected actions of individuals.[23]

Given the unequivocal nature of Hayek's opposition to socialism in all its myriad forms, one might naturally expect him to articulate a decisive answer to the familiar question "how much government is too much." Indeed, knowing of Hayek's opposition to a wide roster of welfarist public policies, one approaches Hayek's work anticipating that he will provide a laundry list of official do's and don'ts. Popularly regarded as one of the leading exponents of the libertarian position, one expects to find a defense of a principle of nonintervention, an argument for a categorical ban against this or that form of state coercion. Surprisingly, however, in his political and philosophical writings, Hayek makes it clear that a liberal society must be open to considering a broad range of regulatory possibilities as unanticipated social problems arise. In one of his last works, *The Political Order of a Free People*, Hayek issues a particularly clear warning to his libertarian acolytes, cautioning against the appropriation of his work for their cause. Here, he explicitly rejects the notion

> that we regard the enforcement of the law and the defense against external enemies as the only legitimate functions of government. . . .

> Far from advocating such a "minimal state," we find it unquestion-
> able that in an advanced society government ought to use its power
> of raising funds by taxation to provide a number of services which
> for various reasons cannot be provided, or cannot be provided
> adequately, by the market.[24]

In this too-often neglected passage, Hayek goes on to endorse state
provision of roads[25] and publicly financed education,[26] as well as

> building regulations, pure food laws, the certification of certain
> professions, the restrictions on the sale of certain dangerous goods
> (such as arms, explosives, poisons and drugs), as well as some safety
> and health regulations for the processes of production and the pro-
> vision of such public institutions as theatres, sports grounds, etc.[27]

In this regard consider as well the following discussion from *The
Constitution of Liberty* where Hayek describes a hypothetical oasis

> in which somebody has acquired control of the whole water supply
> of an oasis and used this position to exact unusual performances
> from those whose life depends on access to that water. Other
> instances of the same kind would be the only doctor available to
> perform an urgent life-saving operation and similar cases of rescue
> in an emergency where special unforeseeable circumstances have
> placed into a single hand the power of rescue from grave danger.
> They are all instances where I should wish that those in whose
> hands the life of another is placed should be under a moral and legal
> obligation to render the help in their power even if they cannot
> expect any remuneration—though they should of course be entitled
> to normal remuneration if it is in the power of the rescued. It is
> because these services are regarded as rights to be counted upon
> that a refusal to render them except on unusual terms is justly
> regarded as a harmful alteration of the environment and therefore as
> coercion.[28]

Statements like these have been known to shock Hayek's lib⟨
who have often been quick to assume, in the much the same
detractors have, that his writings contain a philosophical defense ⟨.
classical liberal position on public policy. The impression of Hayek as a
hard-core libertarian—one who insists on a fixed and uncompromising
principle of nonintervention—endures, however, only because his work
continues to be known more by reputation than by direct encounter.
Although Hayek indulges the rhetoric of line-drawing, stacking his most
well-known writings with readily excerptable libertarian sound bites,
careful examination tells a very different story. In contrast to his portrayal
as an extremist, in both tone and content much of Hayek's writing is
distinguished by a strong propensity for qualification. As an example, in
a well-known opening passage from *The Constitution of Liberty*, Hayek
confidently and succinctly defines freedom as "the state in which a man
is not subject to coercion by the arbitrary will of another or others."[29]
Less well remembered, however, is the hastily appended caveat that freedom "describes a state which man living among his fellows may hope to
approach closely but can hardly expect to realize perfectly. The task of a
policy of freedom must therefore be to minimize coercion or its harmful
effects, even if it cannot eliminate it completely."[30] The author of *The
Constitution of Liberty*—a work of much greater complexity and lesser
popularity than the unabashedly polemical *The Road to Serfdom*—reveals
himself to be a thinker far more tentative and far less strident than
generally believed.

If Hayek is not the libertarian extremist he is reputed to be, just where
does he draw the line between public power and private rights, and how
exactly does he propose to keep legislative power contained? Rather
than adopting a stance of absolute prohibition, Hayek instead makes the
case, deceptive in its simplicity, that legislation in a liberal regime be
propagated in the form of "general, abstract [rules] equally applicable to
all."[31] Hayek characterizes a regime which conforms to this mandate as
one which respects the "rule of law." For Hayek, the key is to distinguish
legislation from commands, or as he explains the point in *The Road to
Serfdom*, to appreciate the significance of the distinction "between laying

down a rule of the Road, as in the Highway code, and ordering people where to go; or, better still, between providing signposts and commanding people which road to take."[32] Thus, Hayek's rule-of-law requirements are intended to insure that laws take the form of "long-term measures, referring to yet unknown cases and containing no references to particular persons, places, or objects."[33] Hayek's approach to limiting government has sometimes been described as a formalist strategy, for rather than naming the specific actions government can and cannot take, Hayek instead proposes a facially neutral standard against which to judge the legitimacy of legislation.[34] In effect, Hayek says that government may do whatever it wishes so long as it does not violate the formal requirements of the rule of law. Hayek shies away from line-drawing, then, in the interest of finding a way beyond the dilemma of neutrality discussed in the first chapter.[35] Recall that for liberals, the point of limiting government is, after all, to prevent the use of state coercion for the pursuit of particularistic aims. Any principle of non-intervention which names or implies specific limits on official power will readily be seen to privilege one inherently controversial theory of fundamental rights over another, thereby undercutting the purpose of imposing limits on government in the first place.

Although Hayek's approach may appeal to liberals concerned with the problem of neutrality, this is not the explanation Hayek gives for his resort to a formal theory of the rule of law. Hayek emphasizes not so much in philosophical commitment to neutrality, as his desire to accommodate the inevitable need for legislative discretion which arises as government seeks to respond to unforeseen contingencies. From Hayek's point of view, the problem with presettling limits on government is that there is no way for society to respond to the unexpected. As an evolutionary theorist who believes that spontaneous orders are superior to planned societies, Hayek worries about the dangers posed in hamstringing the legislature on the basis of a principled opposition to certain sorts of public policies. While he is acutely aware of the potential for legislatures to abuse their discretionary power, at the same time Hayek recognizes the importance of flexibility in a world marked by pervasive and ineliminable uncertainty. Hayek's challenge, then, is to establish limits that are rigorous enough to prevent government from taking ill-considered acts in the present, but which are flexible enough to allow for innovative responses to unanticipated developments in the future. Thus, in yet another passage likely to unsettle his libertarian admirers, Hayek defends a version of the rule of law he hopes will provide

> ample scope for experimentation and improvement within the permanent legal framework which makes it possible for a free society to operate most efficiently. . . . The continuous growth of wealth and technological knowledge which such a system makes possible will constantly suggest new ways in which government might render services to its citizens and bring such possibilities within the range of the practicable.[36]

Limited Government and the Problem of Indeterminacy

In challenging the depiction of Hayek as a libertarian extremist, I have emphasized his refusal to presettle the question of the appropriate scope and reach of legislative power in a liberal regime. Instead, as I have explained earlier, Hayek proposes that legislatures be accorded the discretion to propagate any law which conforms to his rule-of-law requirements, particularly the injunction that laws take the form of "general, abstract rules" that are "equally applicable to all." The urgent question is just how rigorous and effective a constraint this standard is likely to be in practice. Resoundingly, commentators from across the political spectrum have condemned Hayek's approach, placing Hayek in the unenviable position of being the kind of liberal no liberal seems to like. Dissatisfaction with Hayek's approach to limiting government is rooted in a consensus that his rule-of-law standard is at once too restrictive and too permissive. On the one hand, the generality requirement in particular seems to prohibit the passage of virtually any legislation at all, for what law truly can be said to be general in its application? Even laws regulating traffic or prohibiting murder are unacceptable if the generality requirement is interpreted literally, for all laws, including uncontroversial ones such as these, create classes by their very nature, that is, distinguishing murderers from people who do not kill, or people who drive over 65 mph from those who drive more slowly. Alternatively, the generality requirement may be given a less literalistic interpretation, and understood simply to prohibit the passage of laws intended to target, either for sanction or reward, classes or individuals whose identity is known in advance to those authorizing the law. When generality is given this interpretation, however, the Hayekian rule-of-law seems to be too permissive to satisfy Hayek's own demand for governmental restraint. Indeed, as some of Hayek's libertarian critics have emphasized, it seems possible for many regulatory policies to satisfy the criteria the rule of law and yet be illiberal. Political theorist Chandran Kukathas observes that "it is not clear that the abstract and general rules which conform to the ideal of the rule of law will always occur with principles which Hayek, and liberals generally, would find morally acceptable."[37] Historian Ronald Hamowy goes further, suggesting that Hayek's approach might actually be appropriated as a justification for coercion:

> Hayek's proposed framework . . . offers a rationale for what clearly are coercive acts of the state, e.g. conscription, interference in the economy (under the principle that it is attempting to minimize personal coercion) and alteration by fiat of the social structure of personal relationships which have developed spontaneously and undirected over the course of centuries.[38]

It is not just libertarians who have remarked upon the open-endedness of Hayekian constraints on the legislative power as evidence of Hayek's failure to achieve his own aims. Political theorist Richard Flathman concludes that "no satisfactory way of formulating a logical criterion for determining when a law is general in the appropriate (formal) sense has been discovered."[39] And legal and political theorist Cass Sunstein declares that "the rule of law, standing by itself, does not provide [the] theory" that could enable us to distinguish "arbitrary state intervention in the free market from acceptable forms of regulation."[40]

In portraying the ambiguity of Hayek's legislative constraints as a fatal flaw in his thinking, critics assume that since Hayek favors laissez-faire social and economic policies, he must intend for the rule of law to restrict government to passing only the kinds of policies he favors. If this is the case, the thinking goes, Hayek must assume that his rule-of-law criteria will be interpreted against a background theory of rights, one which limits in advance the kind of policies legislatures may consider. For example, Bellamy contends that the only way Hayek can give "determinate content" to the rule of law is by "surreptitiously drawing on the sort of substantive moral reasoning he disavows."[41] Along similar lines, intellectual historian Andrew Gamble suggests that "since Hayek believes that the state must retain some coercive powers, the question of the scope of these power is left indeterminate. It is a practical question to be decided case-by-case. Hayek assumes that the legislators in his ideal constitution will embrace a liberal political philosophy. But he offers no reason why they should."[42] Encapsulating the critical consensus on this point, philosopher John Gray declares that "Hayek's theory is at the very least radically incomplete . . . inasmuch as his conception of the rule of law will have the classical liberal implications he expects of it, only if it incorporates a conception of individual rights, which he seems explicitly to disavow."[43] I would suggest, however, that the critics have made a grave error in assuming, as Gray puts it, that Hayek "expects" the rule of law to have "classical liberal implications." Although critics such as those reviewed typically present their revelations of the permissiveness of the generality requirement as the revelation of a fatal flaw, Hayek himself was well aware of the modesty of constraints the generality requirement imposes on government. In *The Constitution of Liberty*, Hayek notes that "no entirely satisfactory criterion has been found that would always tell us what kind of classification is compatible with equality before the law."[44] Still, he cautions against the conclusion that the rule of law is therefore "meaningless."[45] Instead, he offers a series of further considerations liberal lawmakers should take into account in determining the ultimate desirability of proposed legislation. For example, he suggests that legislators ask whether "those inside any group singled out acknowledge the legitimacy of the distinction as well as those outside it."[46]

While these inquiries suggest guidelines for deliberation, they do not amount to hard-and-fast rules for determining the legitimacy of legislation. Realizing that liberal principles only go so far in proscribing the scope of political power, Hayek believes that it will often be necessary to move beyond the question of what the rule of law allows and to consider on a case-by-case basis the likely outcome of adopting a particular public policy. As he acknowledges, "the observation of the rule of law is a necessary, but not yet a sufficient, condition for the satisfactory working of a free economy."[47] For this reason, Hayek supplements his philosophical argument with substantive policy discussions. However, perhaps assuming that Hayek's policy excursions are offered merely to illustrate his philosophical argument, political theorists have tended to neglect these discussions, giving barely a mention, for example, to the entire second half of *The Constitution of Liberty* in which Hayek presents a series of extended policy discussions on topics ranging from housing to public schools to health care to resource management. To be sure, Hayek's policy discussions assume a background commitment to the rule of law as he defines it, but this is quite clearly only a point of departure; for Hayek, policy analysis picks up where philosophy leaves off. As he explains, the rule of law "provides the criterion which enables us to distinguish between those measures which are and those which are not compatible with a free system." Crucially, however, Hayek goes on to say that "those [policies] that are may be examined further on the grounds of expediency. Many such measures will, of course, still be undesirable or even harmful."[48] And as it turns out, in Hayek's view the problem with most governmental measures is not that they violate the rule of law, but rather that

> the great majority of governmental measures which have been advocated in [the field of economic policy] are, in fact, inexpedient, either because they will fail or because their costs will outweigh the advantages. This means that, so long as they are compatible with the rule of law, they cannot be rejected out of hand as government

intervention but must be examined in each instance from the viewpoint of expediency.[49]

This begs the question: what does Hayek mean by "expediency?" Is this a way of sneaking unspoken standards (like a background theory of rights) back in under the cover of objective policy analysis? After all, expediency must be assessed relative to some set of ends the policies in question are designed to achieve, but Hayek wants to avoid the use of laws to achieve social goals. This leads Gray to suggest that Hayek is a sort of "indirect utilitarian," one who in the end does allow society to adopt and pursue certain broad social aims, as long as these ends are not pursued in an overly forced and inflexible fashion. But even here Gray may be exaggerating Hayek's commitment to specific ends, for although Hayek thinks that the standard of expediency should guide public policy deliberations, he does not insist that this be the case in a liberal society. In the last instance, liberal subjects are free to choose whatever policies they wish, even exceptionally unwise ones, so far as these laws meet the minimum threshold of legitimacy established by rule-of-law constraints.

The point is that Hayek recognizes an important distinction between laws which are illiberal and laws which are unwise, and he urges those committed to combatting coercion to turn their attention away from a search for categorical principles of restraint and toward the kind of nuts-and-bolts policy research that will demonstrate what he takes to be the folly of most social justice legislation. However enticing the promise of line-drawing may be—understood as the assertion of presettled, absolute prohibitions against coercive acts of government—Hayek recognizes that categorical bans are fundamentally illiberal in their very nature, resting as they inevitably must on controversial conceptions of individual rights. Hayek is thus led to fault his libertarian colleagues for failing to see that "the habitual appeal to the principle of non-interference in the fight against all ill-considered or harmful measures [has] had the effect of blurring the fundamental distinction between the kinds of measures which are and those which are not compatible with a free system."[50] As far as Hayek is concerned, foolish policies should be dismissed simply because they are foolish, and in most cases, there will be neither cause nor need to invoke higher-order liberal principles.

Hayek's Institutional Turn

Following the publication of *The Constitution of Liberty* with the *Law, Legislation, and Liberty* trilogy, Hayek sought to augment his formal theory of the rule of law with a plan to redesign the central institutions of democratic government. The significance of Hayek's institutional turn as a critical complement to the rule of law has been downplayed by many critics, who present the revelation of the indeterminacy of the rule-of-law requirements as a critical coup de grace. But rather than vesting exclusively in the rule of law to produce liberal outcomes, Hayek seeks institutional reforms which he hopes will deliver the kind of policy outcomes he favors. However, it should be noted that there is an obvious irony in Hayek's turn to the task of institutional design. Though Hayek is known as a staunch enemy of the planned economy, in the end he advocates for what amounts to planned politics. As economist James Buchanan observes, Hayek gives no compelling reason why we should trust evolution when it comes to regulating the market and social life, while resorting to social engineering in the political arena.[51] Hayek's institutional turn is especially unexpected given his avowed skepticism about political planning in general. In *The Constitution of Liberty*, Hayek makes a point of denying credit to perhaps the most successful constitutional architects history has ever known, the founders of the U.S. Constitution. He opines:

> Much is sometimes made of the fact that the American constitution is the product of design and that, for the first time in modern history, a people deliberately constructed the kind of government under which they wished to live. . . . This attitude . . . was more justified here than in many similar instances, yet still is essentially mistaken. It is remarkable how different from any clearly foreseen structure is the frame of government which ultimately emerged, how much

of the outcome was due to historical accident or the application of inherited principles to a new situation. What new discoveries the federal Constitution contained either resulted from the application of traditional principles to particular problems or emerged as only dimly perceived consequences of general ideas.[52]

Hayek's insistence on the need for institutional reform in liberal democratic regimes like the United States and Great Britain, despite what he recognizes to be the perils of such an undertaking, reflects his profound distrust of majoritarian politics—and his belief that the task of limiting government should be conceived primarily in terms of limiting democracy. Although it is an article of public faith in the United States that free markets and democratic self-government are mutually support-ing, even, perhaps, entailed by each other, Hayek insists that democracy poses grave threats to economic and other liberties. Unlike many modern liberal theorists, then, who downplay the inherent tension between lib-eralism and democracy, Hayek unabashedly proclaims his deep misgiv-ings about their ultimate compatibility. His disdain emanates in a sense that the lofty ideal of self-sovereignty has in the modern age degener-ated into little more than an institutionalized system of interest group pandering. In *The Political Order of a Free People*, Hayek issues a sustained critique of democracy as practiced throughout the twentieth century in the United States, concluding that "we have under the false name of democracy created a machinery in which not the majority decides, but each member of the majority has to consent to many bribes to get major-ity support for his own special demands."[53] In other words, a system that was meant to serve the common good is now merely a scheme of benefits for special interests. Hayek declares: "Under the prevailing sys-tem it is not the common opinion of a majority that decides on common issues, but a majority that owes its existence and power to the gratifying of the special interests of numerous small groups, which the representa-tives cannot refuse to grant if they are to remain a majority."[54] In his view, "democracy needs even more severe restraints on the discretionary powers government can exercise than other forms of government, because it is much more subject to effective pressure from special interests, perhaps of small numbers, on which its majority depends."[55] Although Hayek is hardly alone in assailing the prominent role played by interest groups in modern democracy, he stands apart from those who share his critical stance in refusing to adopt an attitude of hopefulness regarding the return to democracy in a more pure form.

In his writings on democracy, Hayek traces the problem of excessive coercion to a failure to limit legislative power in particular. Too often, he suggests, rule by the people has been mistakenly understood to imply that there can be no limits placed on the will of majoritarian legislatures. Risking heresy in a society that prides itself on its democratic heritage, Hayek takes aim against the deeply rooted assumption that legislation which originates in the will of the people deserves to be accorded the status of law. Hayek attributes this reflexive view to "the pernicious principle of parliamentary sovereignty" bequeathed to the Americans by their British forebearers, and he calls on his contemporaries to relinquish once and for all this baleful legacy.[56] Against those who assume that legislation which originates in a democratic decision-making process is by definition legitimate, Hayek counters that legislation with a democratic pedigree is more likely to show a disregard for the general welfare than laws emanating from more authoritarian systems. Limits on legislative power support rather than undermine democracy by setting constraints on what special interests can hope to attain. Advocating for lowered ambitions, Hayek concludes that the only sustainable democracy is limited democracy. Nonetheless, in the end Hayek resolves that democracy "is an ideal worth fighting for to the utmost, because it is our only protection (even if in its present form not a certain one) against tyranny."[57] But even Hayek's show of support for democracy never moves beyond an instrumental justification, one delivered with a serious qualification: "I do not regard majority rule as an end but merely as a means, or perhaps even the least evil of those forms of government from which we have to choose."[58] While worth preserving, democracy "is far from being the highest political value, and an unlimited democracy may well be worse than limited government of a different kind."[59] Nonetheless, while seeing no intrinsic reason to prefer a law made by a democratic legislature to one handed down from above, Hayek does pledge allegiance to some form of democratic governance, becoming especially spirited in his defense of democracy against what he sees as a rising tide of elitist conservatism.[60] Still, he verges on damning democracy with faint praise, likening it to "sanitary precautions against the plague," a deeply flawed form of rule whose main advantage is that it may prevent the ascendance of something even worse.[61] Finally, while conceding the value of many of the processes and practices associated with democracy, Hayek insists that the term itself be abandoned, preferring instead to use the phrase "demarchy," which he hopes will simultaneously convey his respect for the promise of the democratic ideal while allowing him to take as much distance as possible from the reality of modern democratic government.[62]

In seeking to reform the central institutions of a liberal regime, Hayek suggests that the best way to contain the influence of special interests is to strictly divide the legislative process into two phases, separating the task of identifying general legislative objectives from the job of determining specific policies. In *The Political Order of a Free People*, Hayek offers a model constitution which includes a plan to redistribute legislative power between a Legislative Assembly and a Governmental Assembly. In his proposed scheme, the Legislative Assembly acts by "committing itself to universal rules intended to be applied in an unknown number of future instances and over the application of which to particular cases it has no further power."[63] In giving specific form to these general agreements, the Governmental Assembly is obligated to stay within the bounds created by these mandates. Moving beyond the usual purview of political theorists interested in democratic institutions, Hayek advances an unusual plan for electing members to the Governmental Assembly, opining that "it would seem wise to rely on the old experience that a man's contemporaries are his fairest judges and to ask each group of people of the same age once in their lives, say in the calendar year in which they reached the age of 45, to select from their midst representatives to serve for fifteen years."[64] To further promote responsible decision making,

Hayek proposes that members of each class should be encouraged to mix throughout their adult life in local clubs which, Hayek explains, "would possibly be more attractive if men of one age group were brought together with women two years or so younger."[65] It is a testament to his recognition of the importance of culture and institutions in maintaining a liberal society, however misguided he may be in the specifics, that Hayek considers policies such as these, though he has suffered significant ridicule for straying into such territory.

Hayek's division of duties between the Legislative and Governmental Assemblies can be read as a belated attempt to reign in the wide scope for legislative discretion engendered by the indeterminacy of the rule of law. In *The Constitution of Liberty*, Hayek advances the view that government can only rule by general law, but he struggles to fix a definition of generality that is at once rigorous enough to preclude coercive legislation without at the same time becoming so stringent as to prevent intervention when necessary. The creation of two distinct assemblies promises to alleviate the problem by dividing the legislative process into two stages. In so doing, Hayek hopes to prevent legislators from succumbing to interest group pressures. Legislators, he reasons, are in a position to abuse their power only if they are able to predict the consequences of the rules they make. But if legislators are limited to authoring general rules, they cannot distribute favors or give preferential treatment, nor can they execute specific plans. Of course, this also means that legislators have only a very limited ability to make commitments to their constituents regarding the passage of specific measures, and it also makes it difficult for constituents to assess the efficacy of their representatives. But in Hayek's view, interest-group pandering is simply the flip side of electoral accountability, and if one wishes to minimize the former it may be necessary to sacrifice the latter as well.

Hayek's proposed institutional reforms generally have met with derision, easily dismissed as the whimsical speculations of a doddering professor. Those who have seriously engaged his proposals have been largely unimpressed. In dismissing Hayek's suggestions as outlandish, however, critics have overlooked the extent to which Hayek's proposals are premised on an implicit concession of the irreducible significance of democratic politics in a liberal regime, given the limitations of the rule of law as a constraint on legislative power. In typical fashion, Bellamy lambastes Hayek for aspiring to "dethrone politics," ignoring the fact that Hayek's institutional proposals, though unusual and likely insufficient, attest to his recognition of the need to reinvigorate the democratic process in liberal societies.

While Bellamy worries that Hayek endeavors to constrain the political process, political theorist William Scheuerman goes even further, warning that Hayek aspires to dismantle democracy altogether. In an essay exploring Hayek's affinities with German legal theorist and Nazi collaborator Carl Schmitt, Scheuerman contends that Schmitt and Hayek share more in common than Hayek's liberal admirers would like to believe. In Scheuerman's reading, the main difference dividing these two thinkers is simply the fact that Schmitt is willing to acknowledge that lawmaking is fundamentally "decisionistic" in nature, whereas Hayek obfuscates the question of how decisions about the deployment of political power in a liberal regime are made by hiding behind an ambiguously defined generality requirement. Observing that "some versions of Hayek's definition of general law suggest that virtually any form of state intervention is incompatible with general law, whereas others provide at least some room for welfare state-type activities,"[66] Scheuerman suggests that Hayek seeks to exploit this indeterminacy by opportunistically bending the meaning of the generality requirement "so as to accord with the immediate imperatives of the political struggle against defenders of the welfare state."[67] In other words, Scheuerman accuses Hayek of invoking a rigorous interpretation of the generality rule when he wants to argue for the illegitimacy of a particular measure, but softening its meaning when a policy Hayek considers innocuous or expedient is at stake. In Scheuerman's view, the indeterminacy of the generality requirement gives those in a position of power virtually unfettered discretion, all the while enabling the rhetoric of conformity to the rule of law to serve as a cloak of legitimacy.

Scheuerman makes a salutary contribution in drawing critical attention to the question of the way legislative decisions are to be made in

Hayek's ideal liberal regime, rather than simply assuming that in seeking to dethrone politics, Hayek aims to compress the space for political decision making as much as possible. But should we conclude, as Scheuerman does, that Hayek's distrust of democracy implies a hidden preference for authoritarianism? Recalling Hayek's proposal that the Legislative Assembly be elected in a one-time vote by a single age cohort, Scheuerman wonders "whether Hayek's model deserves to be considered compatible with the basic ideals of modern liberal democracy" at all.[68] Scheuerman concludes that it does not, emphasizing that Hayek's model "would undoubtedly result in a vast reduction of existing possibilities for democratic participation."[69] In likening Hayek to an authoritarian thinker such as Schmitt, however, Scheuerman fails to appreciate the extent to which a commitment to democracy in fact demands a radical rethinking of contemporary political procedures and practices. As an example, consider that Scheuerman takes umbrage at Hayek's suggestion that voting rights for representatives of the Legislative Assembly be restricted, but he ignores the fact that at the same time Hayek seeks to deepen and enrich the social context in which participation occurs, fostering a sense of community intended both to encourage participation and to improve the quality of citizen input. In depicting Hayek's plan as "a vast reduction of existing possibilities for democratic participation," Scheuerman uncritically equates democracy with voting, a move that itself reflects a highly impoverished view of what democratic citizenship means and entails.[70] Were Hayek's proposals to be instituted, perhaps some citizens would be moved to participate in new and more meaningful ways, inspired by an institutional reform that shows promise of untethering government from the yoke of special interests. Or perhaps not, but the question is at least worthy of debate. Rather than condemning those who question the status quo, we do better to encourage those willing to consider democratic reform to push the question of institutional change to a more sophisticated level.

That said, in suggesting that Scheuerman's critique of Hayek is unfair, I do not mean to say that Hayek's proposed innovations should be regarded as impervious to engaged critique. Whereas Scheuerman thinks that Hayek goes too far in tampering with democracy, I would suggest that Hayek does not go far enough. Recall that Hayek advocates for a two-tiered legislature, where power is divided between a Legislative Assembly that passes general laws and a Governmental Assembly that chooses policies consistent with these principles. But because Hayek's rule of law constraints are so vague, very little can be definitively excluded from consideration by the Governmental Assembly. As Hayek himself explains, "the rule of law provides the criterion which enables us to distinguish between those measures which are and those which are not compatible with a free system. Those that are may be examined further on the grounds of expediency."[71] The urgent question, then, is whether Hayek's institutional innovations are sufficient to insure that the deliberations at the level of the Governmental Assembly will proceed in a way that is substantially better than what we have now. Here, Hayek would have done well to take his institutional reforms further. For while he shuffles power around, in the end little is likely to change. As Hamowy observes, "the effect of such a division of powers would be (and, indeed, was) to place in the hands of the lower house all substantive power to govern; for, while it could pick and choose which rules of conduct enacted by the upper house it wished to enforce, it could further enforce its own rules via the taxing power."[72] If Hamowy is right, Hayek should have moved to address the thorny question of how to improve the quality of legislative decision making at the parliamentary stage. Given that Hayek is unwilling to impose significant pre-settled constraints on legislative power while at the same time refusing to dismantle majoritarian legislatures, in the final analysis Hayek is guilty not so much of embracing authoritarianism but of failing to follow through on his own commitment to democracy. Rather than facing the enduring significance of democracy in his ideal regime, Hayek retreats into denial. He suggests that the "further examination" of the possible public policies allowed by the rule of law will somehow proceed in a better way in his ideal regime than it does now, despite the fact that the Governmental Assembly is explicitly modeled on present day parliaments. But if a significant place remains for legislative politics, then Hayek cannot avoid the task of thinking about ways to promote better forms of democratic deliberation. He tries to duck this task with his harsh anti government rhetoric, but the very permissiveness of his rule of law ensures ample room for legislative discretion. Hayek's theory of limits is deficient, then, not because his rule of law does too little, but because he does not supplement it with an adequate theory of the political process. Hayek went in the right direction by looking at institutional reform; he just didn't go far enough, caught between his fear of democracy and his recognition of its necessarily central place in a liberal regime.

Conclusion

Hayek's own rhetoric is at least partly to blame for obscuring the important place his liberalism leaves for democratic politics. In the concluding book of his *Law, Legislation, and Liberty* series, Hayek issues this grim assessment:

> It can scarcely be doubted that quite generally politics has become much too important, much too costly and harmful, absorbing much too much mental energy and material resources, and that at the same time it is losing more and more the respect and sympathetic support of the public at large who have come to regard it increasingly as a necessary but incurable evil that must be borne.[73]

Despite such statements, I have sought to show that Hayek is not antipolitical nor is he antidemocratic, in the sense of advocating radical constraints on the discretionary powers of democratically accountable legislatures. The Hayek depicted here, then, is neither a closet authoritarian nor a staunch libertarian, but rather a reluctant democrat, one whose true failure lies in the denial of the depth of his own commitment to the project of democracy.

CHAPTER THREE

Liberalism and the Justice of Limits

In volume two of Hayek's *Law, Legislation, and Liberty* trilogy, provocatively entitled *The Mirage of Social Justice*, the author pronounces the popular notion of "social justice" a sham, a "superstition," nothing more than a "hollow incantation."[1] Hayek goes on to declare "social justice" to be "empty and meaningless,"[2] dismissing it as "a universally used expression which to many people embodies a quasi-religious belief."[3] In Hayek's judgment, the term "social justice" has "no content whatsoever," and its continued invocation must be regarded as "either thoughtless or fraudulent."[4] Hayek believes that the popularity of the idea of "social justice" rests on the mistaken assumption that a society is capable of exercising the kind of agency which can be properly attributed only to individuals. According to Hayek, justice only may be "predicated about the intended results of human action but not about circumstances which have not deliberately been brought about by men."[5] Just as it would be absurd, for example, to speak of the justice of the laws of nature, given that gravity is neither just nor unjust but simply is, similarly it is nonsensical to speak of a just or an unjust society. In Hayek's view, talk of social justice only makes sense in the context of a command society in which some kind of "directing authority" seeks to realize particular ends. But in a free society—one in which the government is constrained to act through general, abstract rules, it is inappropriate to speak of "social justice" because there is no directing authority, only autonomous individuals pursuing their own aims within a general framework of rules.

Hayek published *The Mirage of Social Justice* in 1976, just five years after the appearance of Rawls's landmark treatise *A Theory of Justice*. Rawls presents his book, explicitly and unapologetically, as a work of social justice. For this reason alone, one would expect Hayek to look upon *A Theory of Justice* with disdain. Instead, in the preface to *The Mirage of Social Justice*, Hayek goes out of his way to say that he takes Rawls to be advocating for a view that is "more or less" the same as his own.[6] Professing a willingness to look beyond what he takes to be nothing more than an unfortunate choice of terminology, Hayek declares the differences dividing him from Rawls to be "more verbal than substantial."[7] Hayek's conclusion is unexpected, to say the least. How could the author of *The Road to Serfdom* possibly endorse the writings of a thinker like Rawls whose project has been described as "the most comprehensive effort in modern philosophy to justify a socialist ethic?"[8] How could a staunch libertarian possibly embrace the position adopted by one of the twentieth century's most influential defenders of the welfare state?

Perhaps the answer lies in Hayek mistaking a passing convergence for a more profound agreement. In explaining his affinity with Rawls, Hayek declares that he

> has no basic quarrel with an author who . . . acknowledges that the task of selecting specific systems or distributions of desired things as just must be "abandoned as mistaken in principle, and it is, in any case, not capable of a definite answer." Rather, the principles of justice define the crucial constraints which institutions and joint activities must satisfy if persons engaging in them are to have no complaints against them. If these constraints are satisfied, the resulting distribution, whatever it is, may be accepted as just (or at least not unjust).[9]

In other words, Hayek sees himself and Rawls as united in the view that a liberal theory of justice prohibits government from mandating this or that particular allocation of resources. Although Rawls is sometimes assumed to be a proponent of redistribution, Hayek recognizes that

Rawls argues for the pursuit of a just allocation of resources only by the indirect means of arranging the basic institutions of society such that just distributions will result.[10]

Is this point of convergence enough to justify Hayek's enthusiasm for Rawls's theory? The very fact that most commentators have failed to remark upon Hayek's endorsement perhaps suggests an unspoken consensus that the elderly Hayek, writing in the twilight of his scholarly career, simply misunderstood Rawls's message. Waldron is one of the very few critics who have commented upon Hayek's affirmation of Rawls, but he quickly dismisses Hayek as "mistaken," rooting the error in the fact that Hayek "exaggerates the implications of Rawls's refusal to consider the justice of particular allocations of goods."[11] What Hayek overlooks, in Waldron's view, is the fact that while opposing post hoc efforts at corrective reallocation, Rawls nonetheless argues for a theory of justice according to which "we are *required* as a matter of justice" to rearrange the basic institutional structure if it is possible to do so in such a way that a more just allocation will result.[12] Without denying that Hayek and Rawls agree that reallocation is an illegitimate strategy for pursuing social justice, Waldron emphasizes their underlying disagreement on the question of whether social justice is itself a legitimate end for society to pursue. On Waldron's reading, far from insisting—as Rawls does—that the basic institutions of a liberal society be arranged so that "social and economic inequalities are to the greatest benefit of the least advantaged," Hayek deems this sort of institutional engineering antithetical to liberalism.

However, in the previous chapter I contested the widely held perception of Hayek as a thinker who, in the words of Waldron, "devoted a large part of his life to arguing . . . that the modern regulated welfare state is incompatible with the rule of law."[13] Without denying Hayek's adamant opposition to redistributive public policies, I sought to establish that Hayek's formulation of the rule of law in fact allows for the passage of all sorts of welfarist legislation, and that it is a recognition of the limitations of the rule of law as a bar to redistribution which leads Hayek to urge institutional reforms, as well as to engage in policy debates which center on questions of efficiency, not justice. In widening his strategy for limiting government beyond a call for conformity to the rule of law, Hayek implicitly concedes the need to supplement the limits on legislation entailed by liberal principles if welfarist legislation is to be avoided. Building on this argument, I would now suggest that far from exaggerating a minor point of agreement, Hayek quite rightly recognizes Rawls to be a kindred spirit in the sense that they share a recognition of the inherent limits of liberal principles to constrain legislative outcomes. Although Hayek could not possibly have been unaware of Rawls's preference for egalitarian social and economic policies, he nonetheless appreciates Rawls's restraint in defining the specifics of an ideal liberal regime. As Hayek correctly discerns, Rawls concedes that liberal principles are in themselves incapable of resolving most of the questions at the heart of political debate in a liberal regime, including matters as basic as whether capitalism or socialism is most consistent with core liberal values. While Hayek and Rawls clearly have different ideas about the desirable level of governmental intervention in everyday life, then, neither of them claims that these preferences are entailed by a commitment to liberal principles alone. It is this agreement which lies at the very heart of the liberal project but which has been obscured in the scholarly discourse on twentieth-century liberalism, especially by those who position Hayek and Rawls as exemplars of competing poles on the liberal continuum, overlooking the underlying fact that neither thinker engages in the sort of line-drawing assumed to lie at the heart of the liberal mission.

John Rawls: Liberal Renegade or Redeemer?

Almost from the moment in 1971 when it first appeared, Rawls's *A Theory of Justice* has served as the reference point for scholarly discussions of Anglo-American liberal political thought in the postwar era. In addition to *A Theory of Justice*, Rawls's major works include *Political Liberalism* (1993) and *Justice as Fairness: A Restatement* (2001). In his post-*Theory* writings, Rawls elaborates and in many instances revises his original argument, but his focus always remains the same: to defend a view of liberal principles of justice which he believes are capable of guiding the exercise of political power, or, as he puts it, to specify "the fair terms of social cooperation" from a liberal point of view.[14] Today, Rawls enjoys a reputation as a champion of the welfare state, and he is credited with producing a compelling philosophical justification for redistributive public policies. Certainly, the sheer heft of the critical literature on Rawls lends credibility to the widely held view that he is "the most important political philosopher of the second half of the 20th century."[15] In the U.S. academy, it is now a standard rite of passage for political theorists of all stripes to reckon with Rawls, and it is a powerful testament to the rigor and complexity of Rawls's thinking that his ideas have been able to bear such intense and sustained scholarly scrutiny. Of course, credit is due as well to Rawls's tireless critics, for it can be fairly said that Rawls demands a great deal of his readers. As Thomas Nagel gently notes, Rawls's books are "very different" from the "rhetorical masterpieces" produced by canonical liberals of yore.[16]

Rawls has done more than any thinker of his era to revive interest in and respect for the liberal position, but he is in important ways an unorthodox liberal, challenging some of the most well-established and deeply cherished axioms associated with the liberal tradition. It is, then, in some respects remarkable that Rawls has been ushered into the liberal canon so readily, given that he offers a controversial and in ways quite radical interpretation of the liberal ideal. Most obviously, Rawls is profoundly critical of his classical liberal forebearers who have taken the protection of private property to be liberalism's central ambition. As political theorist Brian Barry observes, Rawls's theory of justice is "a statement of liberalism which isolates its crucial features by making private property, in the means of production, distribution and exchange, a contingent matter rather than an essential part of the doctrine."[17] In modest prose free of the bombast or fanfare one might expect from a thinker defending such a stark position on the question of liberalism's essence, Rawls painstakingly—if at times ploddingly—builds his case for reconceiving liberal priorities.[18] Although historically liberalism has been defined by a pronounced wariness toward state power, in Rawls's rendering of the liberal ideal the emphasis moves from the question of how to limit excessive coercion to the task of establishing the legitimacy of the exercise of state power. And while it is characteristic of many earlier liberals to concede only grudgingly the necessity of government, Rawls is virtually unmatched among canonical liberal figures in his openness to authorizing a massive regulatory regime. Dispensing with the familiar tone of ambivalence common among liberal reflections on the "necessary evil" of government, Rawls seems to happily accept the compatibility of redistributive social and economic policies with core liberal principles.[19] From the standpoint of liberalism, at least as it has been traditionally understood, there is something scandalous about Rawls's receptivity to the possibility of interventionist legislation. But for Rawls, there is a crucial distinction to be drawn between opposition to *big government* and support for *limited government*. While Rawls shares with his liberal forebearers the view that government may act only in ways consistent with underlying commitments to liberty, equality, and respect for individual autonomy, unlike so many of his liberal brethren, Rawls does not believe that these constraints necessitate opposition to welfare state policies like progressive taxation, public schooling, or even centralized health care.

Masking the provocativeness of his claims, especially in the context of a society characterized by an almost automatic suspicion of big government initiatives, Rawls shows a penchant for rhetoric which makes his argument seem—in the words of political theorist Thomas Pogge—"as bland, traditional, and mainstream American as possible."[20] Rather than pitching his work as a radical re-visioning of the liberal theory of limited government, Rawls describes his project in terms of an effort "to specify the terms of social cooperation," a disarming euphemism which obscures the fact that in Rawls's ideal regime it is government which mediates among the individuals who cooperate in society.[21] Rawls's rhetorical choices may have their origins in an effort to downplay the strikingly wide degree of discretion he ultimately accords to government, though in this effort he is not entirely successful. Reading between the lines, political theorist Roberto Alejandro declares himself "struck by the large shadow of the Rawlsian state" in Rawls's ideal political society, leading him to wonder whether there is much room for individual liberty in the Rawlsian regime after all.[22] Similarly, political theorist Bonnie Honig sees an irony in the fact that "in the name of a more democratic politics, [Rawls] recenters the state that other democratic activists are actively involved in decentering."[23] In obscuring, rather than defending, the significance of the role of the state in his ideal regime, Rawls avoids engaging with critics like these who remain less sanguine about the ability to keep governmental oppression in check.

Precisely because of Rawls's renunciation of at least one prominent strand of liberal theory—that associated with a defense of minimal government—one might have expected his intervention to spark an identity crisis for liberals, challenging as Rawls does some of the most fundamental views characterizing liberal thought of the past. Instead, *A Theory of Justice* and Rawls's subsequent writings have largely served a unifying function, standing as an authoritative articulation of a shared set of assumptions around which recent proponents of liberal ideas have rallied. Today, it can be fairly said that the flourishing body of critical scholarship on Rawls serves as a primary site of engagement for ongoing debates about the merits and limitations of the liberal point of view. While useful in providing a venue for scholarly exchange, however, the consensus that Rawls is the exemplary liberal of our times also creates an incentive amongst commentators to downplay the significance of those features of Rawls's approach which are most distinctive, for the more idiosyncratic Rawls's work is considered to be, the less significant the critical commentary surrounding his contribution may seem. In what follows, I suggest that certain crucial features of Rawls's conception of limited government in particular have been misunderstood, obscured in the tidal wave of commentary intent on portraying Rawls as a liberal in the familiar tradition of line-drawing. More specifically, in setting out to identify fundamental principles of justice against which to assess the legitimacy of governmental action, Rawls seems every bit the typical liberal, seeking a pre-political, principled resolution to the question of the scope and reach of official power. Rawls's innovation is commonly assumed to lie in his conclusions about *where* the line between public power and private rights should be drawn, not in his underlying approach to containing legislative power. I will contend, however, that this familiar rendering of the Rawlsian project rests on a misconstrual of

Rawls's resolution to the question of how much government is too much. Though observers commonly depict Rawls as a redistributionist, he does not in fact insist upon the necessity of welfarist policies, instead arguing merely for the legitimacy of redistributive policies should they be authorized through fair democratic decision-making procedures.[24] In drawing attention to Rawls's tentativeness at the level of policy prescriptions, I mean to highlight the significance of the kinds of questions he leaves open for determination in the political process. And in focusing on the wide berth for legislative debate allowed in the ideal Rawlsian regime, I aim to challenge a prominent position represented in the critical literature on Rawls, a position adopted by those who characterize him as "anti-political" due to his avowed goal of deflating the stakes of political debate and diminishing as much as possible the scope of legislative discretion.[25] In addition to challenging the legitimacy of the aspiration to limit the purview of politics, Rawls's critics have gone on to argue that the liberal principles he proposes are in any event far too indeterminate to forestall political controversy, and thus, the Rawlsian regime inevitably is one gripped by precisely the sort of destabilizing political debates he seeks to avoid. In the pages that follow, I offer an alternative account of the role played by indeterminacy in the ideal Rawlsian regime. It is my contention that critics have misconstrued the role that presettled principles of justice play in his ideal regime, for Rawls aims not to preempt political debate, but only to neutralize its effects. As I explain, Rawls strives to achieve this end by framing contention as disagreement not over fundamental questions of justice, but rather over matters of application. Similar to Hayek, Rawls leaves significant room for political debate, begging questions concerning the structure and practice of democratic politics in the ideal liberal regime—questions to which I turn in the second half of the book.

Limited Government in the Rawlsian Regime

What provision does Rawls make for limiting the power of government in his ideal regime? Though he appears to favor policies that would qualify in the eyes of many as a plan for "big government," it would be unfair to suggest that Rawls relinquishes the long-standing liberal commitment to limited government. Like the legions of liberals who have come before him, Rawls is deeply concerned with the problem of coercion in a liberal regime. The difference is this: while in the past liberals have focused on threats to liberty emanating in discrete assertions of power, such as those initiated by individual officials or authorized by political bodies like legislatures or courts, Rawls is centrally concerned with what might be called structural coercion. That is, he is interested in "the way in which the major social institutions distribute fundamental rights and duties and determine the division of advantages from social cooperation."[26] Political philosopher Thomas Nagel offers this useful sketch of Rawls's position:

> Being born the child of slaves or the child of slave-owners, the child of unskilled laborers or the child of wealthy entrepreneurs, is in a sense a matter of pure luck, but the institutions of slavery or capitalism are human creations. And so we can ask ourselves, as members of a society (and ultimately of a world order), whether the conditions for life-governing good and bad luck that our institutions create are morally acceptable.[27]

Because Rawls is so highly attuned to the way in which the underlying institutions and structures constrain individual choices, he concludes that provisions for limiting government must extend to a consideration of the design of what he calls the "basic structure" of society, rather than focusing on the more immediate level of the scope and reach of legislative power.

In *A Theory of Justice*, Rawls sets out to identify the fundamental principles of justice to guide the design of the basic structure of a liberal society. He proposes to derive these principles by way of a thought-experiment based upon an imaginary pre-political choice situation he calls the "original position." As Rawls describes it, the original position is a convention of proto-citizens, subjects stripped down to their essence as "free and equal rational beings." Shrouded behind a blinding "veil of ignorance," subjects are denied access to virtually all forms of self-knowledge, including such basic facts as their sex, race, religion, talents, temperament, and tastes. Rawls deems such information irrelevant to decision-makers charged with selecting the fundamental principles of justice, for in his view, "the natural distribution of assets, abilities and talents" is "arbitrary from a moral point of view."[28] That is, in Rawls's opinion, "there is no more reason to permit the distribution of income and wealth to be settled by the distribution of natural assets than by historical and social fortune."[29] In other words, since no one has a natural right to benefit from the particular attributes with which one happens to be endowed (nor, for that matter, do those less well-endowed deserve to suffer for their bad luck), there is no reason to allow people in the original position to take their own circumstances into account when choosing principles of justice. Challenging one of the most sacred precepts of a society built upon a veneration of the self-made man, Rawls questions the common sense view that those who are, for example, especially intelligent, athletically gifted, or blessed with a higher-than-average capacity for concentration, deserve to receive a greater share of social benefits than those with lesser endowments.[30]

The blinding constraints on self-awareness imposed by the veil of ignorance are intended to guarantee that the decisions made there are the choices "that free and rational persons concerned to further their own interest would accept in an initial position of equality."[31] The point is to ask what sort of system for distributing social benefits each of us would choose if we were deprived of personal knowledge about where we fall on the spectrum of socially recognized talents and skills. Based on the hypothetical deliberations imagined to take place in the original position, Rawls contends that there are two principles to which all rational parties would agree. The first principle, sometimes referred to as the Equal Liberty Principle, has been articulated by Rawls as follows:[32]

> Each person has the same indefeasible claim to a fully adequate scheme of equal basic liberties, which scheme is compatible with the same scheme of liberties for all.

Rawls gives the Equal Liberty Principle priority over his second, and significantly more controversial principle of justice—generally known as the Difference Principle:

> Social and economic inequalities are to satisfy two conditions: first, they are to be attached to offices and positions open to all under conditions of fair equality of opportunity; and second, they are to be to the greatest benefit of the least-advantaged members of society (the difference principle).[33]

In the years since Rawls first introduced the two principles, there has been an enormous amount of scholarly debate concerning whether subjects in an original choice situation would in fact converge on these two ideas. A second line of controversy surrounding the two principles has also attracted significant attention which concerns the question of exactly what these principles entail as a practical matter. What sorts of rights, constitutional or otherwise, are implied by a commitment to the principle of equal liberty? And what kinds of social and economic policies flow from the Difference Principle?

Despite the obvious vagueness of the two principles, Rawls insists that in the ideal liberal regime, all decision-making subsequent to the original position should proceed in terms of an effort to apply or specify the two principles. Rawls envisions this work taking place in three phases following the original position, completing what he calls the "four-stage sequence." Upon exit from the original position, representatives are to proceed to deliberations about constitutional provisions, followed by a legislative stage and finally, an administrative one. Crucially, Rawls declares that at each stage the deliberators—whether they are constitutional architects, legislators, or bureaucrats—are to be bound by the two principles. Thus, at the constitutional stage the task is to design the "most effective just constitution," by which Rawls simply means the one "that satisfies the principles of justice and is best calculated to lead to just and effective legislation."[34] The constitution of the ideal liberal regime is to specify just procedures and just outcomes, with a just procedure defined as rules most likely to generate legislative outcomes that "accord with the two principles of justice."[35] Once a constitution is chosen, Rawls's imaginary subjects advance to the legislative stage. Here, he explains, "proposed bills are judged from the position of a representative legislator who, as always, does not know the particulars about himself. Statutes must satisfy not only the principles of justice but whatever limits are laid down in the constitution."[36] Finally, in the administrative stage, participants are to be concerned with "the application of rules to particular cases by judges and administrators, and the following of rules by citizens generally."[37]

As I alluded earlier, much of the scholarly debate since *A Theory of Justice* has focused on the question of whether rational deliberators in the original position would settle upon the two principles as Rawls defines them. This debate is critical, since the fundamental contention at the heart of Rawls's scheme is that his two principles of justice set the parameters for the legitimate exercise of coercion in the ideal liberal regime. Recognizing what he calls "the fact of reasonable disagreement," Rawls readily acknowledges that in a pluralistic society one should expect to encounter a multitude of differing opinions about what constitutes "the good life"—a philosophical term of art which refers to a bundle of beliefs ranging from views about the role that religion plays in human fulfillment to the question of whether it is better to be rich or happy. As a liberal, Rawls recognizes that "a continuing shared understanding on one comprehensive religious, philosophical, or moral doctrine can be maintained only by the oppressive use of state power."[38] Acknowledging that liberal subjects will endorse a broad array of competing visions about how to live the best life—what Rawls calls differing "comprehensive doctrines"—he nonetheless believes in the existence of an "overlapping consensus" among these comprehensive doctrines regarding the two principles. Somewhat confusingly, he insists that justice as fairness is a "political" rather than a "comprehensive" doctrine in the sense that it rests only upon "shared agreements" about the basic structure of society.[39] The stakes of this claim are high, for if Rawls's theory of justice turns out to be a comprehensive, and hence controversial doctrine, then coercion in the name of the two principles rightfully may be condemned as oppressive by all of those whose views lie outside of the consensus.

Much Ado About Nothing

In an oft-cited passage, Rawls asserts that

"Liberal principles meet the urgent political requirement to fix, once and for all, the content of certain political basic rights and liberties, and to assign them special priority. Doing this takes those guarantees off the political agenda and puts them beyond the calculus of social interests, thereby establishing clearly and firmly the rules of political contest. To regard that calculus as relevant in these matters leaves the status and content of those rights and liberties still unsettled; it subjects them to the shifting circumstances of time and place, and by greatly raising the stakes of political controversy, dangerously increases the insecurity and hostility of public life.[40]

Rawls insists upon establishing "once and for all" guarantees of basic rights and liberties for reasons that are both principled and prudential. On the one hand, Rawls's position reflects his adherence to the standard logic of the liberal social contract, a view which holds that individuals are obligated to submit to government only when public authority derives from the consent of the governed. Decisions made under the ideal conditions of the original position are "the principles that free and rational persons concerned to further their own interests would accept in an initial position of equality as defining the fundamental terms of their association."[41] By insisting that these pre-political agreements not be subject to subsequent review, Rawls seeks to assure that the terms of the social contract will be maintained intact. It is clear from the quoted passage, however, that Rawls bases his preference for presettlement not simply on a commitment to consent. As his statement reveals, Rawls is gravely concerned with the threat that political controversy poses to the stability of the liberal order. In taking certain questions "off of the political agenda," he aims to avoid the kind of political controversy which may disrupt the smooth functioning of a liberal regime.

Rawls's claim to have resolved "once and for all" basic questions of justice rankles commentators who contend that he in effect asks liberal subjects to sacrifice their right to democratic self-governance—understood to involve ongoing debate about fundamental rights—in exchange for a guarantee of a fixed roster of minimum rights. Waldron ventures that it is "not at all clear" that Rawls "actually contemplates disagreements about justice in a well-ordered society."[42] Less cautiously, Bellamy characterizes Rawls's view as the notion that "fundamental" questions about justice "must be completely beyond discussion, and public debate [must] avoid reference to any values that might fall outside the consensus."[43] Gray depicts Rawls as a thinker seeking "escape from the uncertainties and creativity of human judgment."[44] Alejandro describes Rawls's project as an "effort to insulate justice from contingency" by foreclosing political debates about fundamental questions of justice.[45] And political theorist Benjamin Barber characterizes Rawls's project as nothing less than an effort to "subjugate politics to the discipline of philosophy."[46] Establishing a philosophical resolution to basic questions of justice, Rawls seems to reserve for political debate only relatively mechanical matters regarding how to apply the principles in actual practice, creating a modern-day equivalent of rule by philosopher-king, where fidelity to the two principles takes the place of democratic decision-making.[47] On this point, the critics cited above are united in an opposition to line-drawing, contending that political debate, rather than philosophical presettlement, is the appropriate way to make judgments about fundamental matters of justice in a democratic context.

But is it fair to charge Rawls with trivializing politics? Does his scheme preclude the possibility of political debate about "fundamental" questions of justice? Do the two principles of justice provide a "once and for all" settlement to all the important questions likely to arise in a liberal democratic polity? Despite Rawls's reliance on the rhetoric of presettlement, in the remainder of this chapter I suggest that the two principles create enormous room for political debate about matters commonly considered fundamental. As I explain, however, in making this claim I do not subscribe to the common view that Rawls fails in his avowed ambition to deflate the stakes of politics. Instead, Rawls's plan to diffuse political controversy involves a strategic reframing of conflict rather than an effort to banish debate altogether. As I explain further, in characterizing the conflicts likely to arise in the ideal liberal regime as debates over questions of application rather than disagreements about fundamental principles of justice, Rawls endeavors not so much to eliminate controversy as to convince liberal subjects that political disagreements are by their very nature lacking in the degree of significance necessary to justify disruptive expressions of dissent.

To explain, consider first the nature and scope of the questions left open by the two principles at the second stage of Rawls's four stage sequence, the constitutional stage. Here, Rawls asks that we imagine a constitutional convention in which delegates are charged with identifying "constitutional essentials," those features of a liberal constitution which are to include the "fundamental principles that specify the general structure of government and the political process" as well as "equal basic rights and liberties of citizenship that legislative majorities are to respect."[48] Again mobilizing the rhetoric of pre-political settlement, Rawls explains that his intent in establishing constitutional essentials is to take "these guarantees off the political agenda of political parties; it puts them beyond the calculus of social interests, thus securing clearly and firmly the terms of social cooperation on a footing of mutual respect."[49]

Rawls's rhetorical emphasis on the need for firm agreement on constitutional essentials distracts attention from the significant indeterminacy he allows to remain at the level of constitutional deliberation. Note first that Rawls himself anticipates serious debate at the constitutional convention about the specific nature of constitutional essentials; he does not contend that the two principles in and of themselves entail a specific resolution to the question of which rights should be held as basic in a liberal society. Speculating about the likely outcome of constitutional deliberations, Rawls acknowledges that "it is not always clear which of several constitutions, or economic and social arrangements, would be chosen. But when this is so, justice is to that extent likewise indeterminate. Institutions within the permitted range are equally just, meaning that they could be chosen, they are compatible with all the constraints of the theory."[50] Concessions of this sort announced by Rawls have been downplayed, however, by critics intent on portraying Rawls as antipolitical—theorists like Honig who suggest that Rawls's single-minded goal is "to isolate the right vantage point, to establish the right setting, to facilitate the identification of these right resolutions, to dissolve the remainders of politics rather than engage them."[51]

While Rawls insists that agreement on constitutional essentials is necessary to insure political stability and order, he is careful to characterize these agreements in ways which leave ample room for lingering political debate. For example, in *Political Liberalism*, Rawls explains that at the constitutional stage, while there must be agreement on certain basic political rights and liberties such as equal voting rights and freedoms of political speech and association, disagreement is likely to erupt regarding the precise content and boundaries of these rights and liberties, as well as on what further rights and liberties are to be counted as basic and so to merit legal if not constitutional protection. And in *Justice as Fairness*, Rawls offers the equivocal assurance that "on constitutional essentials and matters of basic justice we do try for an agreed basis; so long as there is at least rough agreement here, fair social cooperation among citizens can, we hope, be maintained."[52] From here, he goes on to insist only that there must be "agreement on what those essentials should be, not in every detail, of course, but in the main outlines."[53] Of course, even the distinction between "main outlines" and "details" breaks down with the recognition that the two principles leave unsettled the question of just which rights are to be accorded constitutional protection. Far from reducing the constitutional convention to a mechanical exercise, then, the vagueness of the two principles virtually guarantees wide-ranging debate at the level of constitutional essentials.[54]

It is at this point that some commentators have declared Rawls a failure, judged against the standard of his own stated goals, for it would seem that the indeterminacy of the two principles undermines his effort to eliminate controversy over fundamental questions of justice.[55] For example, Bellamy concludes that the indeterminacy of the two principles "places the basic liberties squarely within the political realm of negotiation and compromise, rather than at a metapolitical level of overlapping consensus where Rawls wishes to remove them."[56] But this conclusion is too hasty. The indeterminacy of the two principles does allow for debate about questions most observers would label fundamental questions of justice, but this indeterminacy does not necessarily lead to the kind of debate that Rawls would consider destabilizing. To understand this point, let us proceed to an examination of the kinds of questions left open for consideration at the legislative stage. Based on Rawls's own pronouncements about "once and for all" settlements, Waldron (like Bellamy) concludes that "the legislature on Rawls's conception is not a place for fundamental disagreements about justice."[57] At first glance, Waldron's contention seems strange, given Rawls's own admission that the Difference Principle is indeterminate on such basic questions as whether the economic order of the ideal liberal regime should be capitalist or socialist, leaving the matter largely open for debate at the legislative stage.[58] Some commentators have taken Rawls's hesitance to resolve basic economic questions as evidence that he views issues of economic equality as less fundamental than matters of equal liberty, and thus, he is happy to allow such relatively unimportant matters to be negotiated in the political process. However, Rawls's unwillingness to fix and settle the implications of the Difference Principle as constitutional essentials should not be taken to imply that he regards the matters it bears upon as unimportant. Indeed, Rawls is emphatic that rights enshrined as constitutional essentials are not to be presumed to be more fundamental than rights established (and subject to change) in the ordinary political process. In his words, "the rights and liberties and procedures included in a constitutional consensus cover but a limited part of the fundamental political questions that will be debated. There are forces tending to amend the constitution in certain ways to cover further constitutional essentials, or else to enact the necessary legislation with much the same effect."[59] In Rawls's view, then, the difference between constitutional essentials and ordinary legislation has only to do with the extent to which it is reasonable to expect agreement on what it is the principles of justice imply in practice. Rawls believes that, unlike in the case of equal liberties, the question of the specific meaning of the Difference Principle is likely to be sufficiently ambiguous as to warrant ongoing political debate. He explains:

> Whether the constitutional essentials covering the basic freedoms are satisfied is more or less visible on the face of constitutional arrangements and how these can be seen to work in practice. But whether the aims of the principles covering social and economic inequalities are realized is far more difficult to ascertain. These matters are nearly always open to wide differences of reasonable opinion; they rest on complicated inferences and intuitive judgments that require us to assess complex social and economic information about topics poorly understood.[60]

Rawls's determination about whether to leave a question open for political debate rests not, then, on a judgment about the degree of importance of the question, but rather on the likelihood that a stable consensus can be established.

Crucially, Rawls does not regard the political process as an improper space for hashing out fundamental questions of justice; rather, he sees it as precisely the place for such debates to occur in those cases in which the two principles are sufficiently indeterminate as to render agreement on particulars unlikely. Contrary to the impression presented by the commentators cited above, Rawls recognizes that disagreements will arise in the just society, even one guided by the two principles of justice. Rawls's point, however, is that these disagreements will concern not the nature of justice itself, but only how to operationalize shared principles. As Waldron himself acknowledges: "Rawls concedes that people do have 'reasonable differences of opinion' about whether legislation is just; but he characterizes those as disagreements about how to apply Rawlsian principles in a complex world, not disagreements about which principles to apply."[61] Interestingly however, in characterizing Rawls's argument this way, Waldron uncritically adopts Rawls's implicit distinction between two types of disagreement, which we might think of as *normative* and *empirical*. Normative disagreement arises from indeterminacy in the meaning of the principles themselves. In cases of normative disagreement, the principles are ambiguous, allowing for a range of possible interpretations. What Waldron refers to as "disagreements about which principles to apply" is a form of normative indeterminacy rooted in confusion about the meaning of Rawls's two principles themselves. Empirical disagreements are different. Here, there is agreement on the question of which principle to apply, but what is lacking is sufficient knowledge about the nature of reality to decisively resolve the question of what course the principle prescribes. As Rawls explains, disagreement of this second, empirical sort, is especially likely to arise when it comes to applying the Difference Principle:

> Now, the question whether legislation is just or unjust, especially in connection with economic and social policies, is commonly subject to remarkable differences of opinion. In these cases judgment frequently depends upon speculative political and economic doctrines and upon social theory generally. Often the best that we can say of a law or policy is that it is at least not clearly unjust. The application of the difference principle in a precise way normally requires more information than we can expect to have. . . .[62]

An example of the sort of disagreement Rawls describes here is the debate over the minimum wage. Consistent with the mandate of the Difference Principle, some argue that in raising the minimum wage, the prospects of the least well-off in society are improved by creating more income for workers. Others, however, believe that minimum wage provisions harm the least well-off because the higher cost to employers leads to more layoffs and fewer job opportunities overall. In this case, the disagreement concerns the application of the Difference Principle, not the merits or meaning of the Difference Principle itself.

Now, in characterizing disagreements at the legislative stage as empirical disagreements—that is, as disagreements rooted in questions of application rather than principle—Rawls makes a move I'll call the empirical dodge. That is, Rawls attributes controversy at the legislative stage to the difficulties that arise when we try to apply general principles to specific situations, rather than to disagreements about fundamental principles of justice (which he claims to have resolved at earlier stages in the sequence). But the very distinction he seeks to draw between indeterminacy arising at the level of principle and indeterminacy arising at the level of practice is arbitrary, for the way we parse indeterminacy—distinguishing disagreements about "justice" from disagreements about "social policy"—ultimately says more about how we choose to view the stakes of the debate than it does about the nature of the disagreement itself. Put otherwise, Rawls's assertion that agreement on the two principles of justice resolves fundamental questions of justice and leaves open only matters of "specification" is a little like saying that antiabortion and pro-choice partisans fundamentally agree that life is sacred, but that they simply disagree on the details—like how to define life and when it begins! In the abortion case, it seems obvious that the significance of an agreement depends on its specificity.

In identifying principles of justice, a society always faces a trade-off: the more general the principles are, the easier it will be to garner agreement for them, but the more likely it is that disagreements will erupt at the application stage. Viewed in this light, the distinction between questions of justice and matters of application reflects a decision about the stage at which conflict is to be confronted, but it tells us nothing about the intrinsic nature or the relative seriousness of the conflict itself. From this perspective, Rawls's effort to distinguish fundamental questions of justice from matters of application looks like a kind of shell game in which he hides and shifts disagreements until they can be dealt with in the least disruptive manner. In this respect, it is useful to consider the notorious ballot controversy that arose following the 2000 presidential election in the United States.[63] Hoping to preempt the chaos of a constitutional crisis, many public officials, as well as those in the media, portrayed the vote counting dispute as a disagreement about details, rather than a conflict over fundamental principles of justice. That is, the prevailing spin on the situation was that while everyone was in agreement with the justice of the principle of "one person, one vote," the disagreement surrounding butterfly ballots concerned only the question of what counts as a vote. Should we count ballots with dimpled chads? Pregnant chads? Hanging chads? In the case of election 2000, construing the controversy as a matter of specification helped to defuse the crisis by limiting the apparent scope of the conflict. But now that the crisis has passed, it is all too easy to forget that those who lost were the ones who claimed that a fundamental principle *was* at stake. From their perspective, it made no sense to talk about a right to vote without settling what it means to vote; the seeming autonomy of these issues is nothing more than an analytic sleight of hand at odds with a reality in which the right to vote is only meaningful so long as it corresponds to a set of agreed upon practices.

As in the vote counting controversy of 2000, when we consider the kinds of disputes likely to emerge in the Rawlsian regime, it looks a lot like we are debating questions which most people would consider fundamental questions of justice: should the economy conform to laissez-faire principles or be redistributionist? Does the official mandate to insure "equality of opportunity" imply a right to universal health care or subsidized higher education? In Rawls's lexicon, such issues may not be referred to as fundamental, but that is only because the term "fundamental" has a special meaning for Rawls, a meaning most people—including most other political theorists—would reject. For Rawls, the designation "fundamental" is not a qualitative attribute but a temporal one, reflecting a judgment about the stage at which an issue is most appropriately confronted, rather than an assessment of the significance of the question itself. Too often, however, the critics who assail Rawls for his avowed goal of prohibiting debate about fundamental questions of justice have been distracted by Rawls's rhetoric and blinded to the significance of the questions that are left open for political resolution in the Rawlsian regime.[64]

This is not to suggest that Rawls's rhetorical choices are insignificant. For Rawls, the advantage of characterizing matters in this way is that positing agreement on fundamental questions promotes stability—even if the agreement turns out to rest on nothing more than the mere assertion of its existence. This point suggests a subtle, but critical shift in the way we read Rawls. Consider in this regard Waldron's observation that Rawls proceeds "*as though* legislative deliberation, in a well-ordered society, could not possibly involve fundamental disagreement about matters of principle, *as though* when we think about the legislative process we should regard all such disagreements of principle as having been settled at an earlier stage (emphasis added)."[65] Although there is a difference between asserting that disagreements *actually have been settled* at an earlier stage, and encouraging us to act *as though* disagreements have been settled, in practice the distinction disappears if the pretense of prior agreement defuses present disagreement.

It is precisely because so much rides on his claim of having achieved agreement on background principles of justice that Rawls chooses to portray the movement from the original position through the constitutional stage and into the legislative stage as one of mere "specification," rather than an ongoing process of debate about fundamental questions of justice. Not only does positing agreement promote stability by encouraging a perspective on controversy that minimizes volatility, but the notion of background agreements also forecloses claims of oppression which might lead to destabilizing forms of resistance. In *Justice as Fairness*, Rawls explains that "the basic structure is arranged so that when everyone follows the publicly recognized rules of cooperation, and honors the claims the rules specify, the particular distributions of goods that result are acceptable as just (or at least as not unjust) whatever these distributions turn out to be."[66] This statement reveals how much Rawls buys in deferring confrontation with disagreements to the application stage. No matter how vague and indeterminate agreed upon principles may be, Rawls insists that the very fact of a background agreement obliges citizens to embrace the legitimacy of the political system.[67]

Conclusion

In the end, Rawls is best understood not as a thinker who proposes a resolution to conflicts over fundamental questions of justice in a liberal regime, but rather as one who seeks to secure a basis for governmental coercion in the face of ongoing disagreements about justice. While the aim of earlier liberals concerned with limited government was to limit coercion consistent with an underlying theory of rights, in Rawls's hands the project of limited government is reoriented around an effort to justify coercion in a pluralistic society. In this regard, Rawls ardently disputes the suggestion that the indeterminacy of the two principles is a "defect," since "justice as fairness will prove a worthwhile theory if it defines the range of justice more in accordance with our considered judgments than do existing theories, and if it singles out with greater sharpness the graver wrongs a society should avoid."[68] But the burning question remains: how should a just society select among a number of competing though "equally just" policies?

To this question, Rawls offers no definitive answer. He merely acknowledges that it is a "problem . . . to select from among the procedural arrangements that are both just and feasible. . . . To solve this problem intelligently requires a knowledge of the beliefs and interests that men in the system are liable to have and of the political tactics that they will find it rational to use given their circumstances."[69] Rawls does not pursue these questions, perhaps content that citizens motivated by a sense of justice will do the right thing, whatever it happens to be. The more likely scenario, of course, is that political questions will be settled roughly as they are now, and that the indeterminacy of the two principles will enable the continued rule of politics as usual.

We are thus led to the conclusion similar to the one arrived at in the preceding analysis of Hayek's approach to limited government: precisely because Rawls leaves such a wide berth for political debate, more attention is due to the question of the nature of democratic process out of which resolutions to political questions emerge. Throughout his writings, Rawls consistently denies the relevance of such considerations, but as I have now shown, for liberal citizens concerned with the extent and nature of the deployment of the state's coercive powers, a focus on the democratic political process, rather than on the nature of pre-political limiting principles, is essential. This is the subject to which I turn in the second half of the book.

CHAPTER FOUR

Liberalism's Legislative Renaissance

At the dawn of a new millennium, liberal theorizing about limited government finds itself at an impasse. Twentieth-century liberal theorists engaged in a fierce debate over the nature of first principles with the hope that arriving at an agreement on core liberal values might finally lead to a resolution of the long-standing controversy concerning how much government is too much. Rather than emerging in a consensus, however, liberals today find themselves deadlocked between libertarians and welfarists. In the previous two chapters, however, I have sought to show that beneath the persistent disagreements dividing liberals lies an implicit recognition that liberal principles alone cannot resolve the question of the legitimate scope and reach of coercion. The surprising renunciation of line-drawing by twentieth-century liberals reflects a shared commitment to respecting pluralism.[1] For liberals, the commitment to pluralism is based on a recognition that there is room for reasonable disagreement about the nature of rights and the legitimate exercise of coercive power. As Bellamy explains, "the basic pluralist belief affirms that there are many moral and non-moral values and that in practice they may prove either inherently or contingently incompatible."[2] In the face of this disagreement, liberals refuse to enshrine substantial settlements into law, recognizing that doing so itself constitutes a form of coercion by imposing a controversial conception of rights upon society as a whole. In this way, what Rawls has dubbed "the fact of pluralism" poses a serious dilemma for liberals, for if agreement on fundamental rights and values is impossible, how can the members of a liberal polity expect to come to an agreement about where the limits of governmental power lie?

Despite a growing consensus that line-drawing is inconsistent with the liberal commitment to respecting pluralism, the pretense of presettlement endures in liberal theory, manifest in the rhetoric permeating the works of thinkers as different as Hayek and Rawls. Perhaps the most alluring aspect of line-drawing for liberals lies in its promise, however mythic, to relieve liberal subjects of the burden of eternal vigilance over government by offering guaranteed rights. In seeming to lower the stakes of everyday politics, the demands liberalism places on its citizens are correspondingly lessened, too, for where lines are fixed and settled, political involvement no longer seems necessary to guard one's rights, but rather becomes a choice available to those who deem participation desirable. Even for those who would not choose to be involved, line-drawing offers the security that certain basic rights will never be open to debate. In turning away from line-drawing, however, liberals leave the question of the legitimate scope and reach of government unsettled, open to negotiation in the political process. For most liberals, who by disposition seem especially attracted to the security promised by line-drawing, the notion of political debate about rights and limits is unsettling, courting the twin threats of instability and oppression. How can individual rights be considered secure if their meaning is constantly open to negotiation in the political process, subject to the whims of legislatures notorious for the tendency toward majority tyranny? How can the very legislatures which pose such risks to individual liberty be charged with determining the reach of their own power? Rather than pursuing answers to these questions, too often liberals have simply ignored the problem, insisting on the rhetoric of line-drawing even in the face of an underlying recognition of the impossibility of substantive presettlement. In the previous two chapters, I argued that such is the case with Hayek and Rawls, for whom maintaining the pretense of line-drawing serves in the last instance merely to discourage attention to—and hence, exploitation of—the discomfiting unboundedness of political power in an ideal liberal regime.

Is there a better approach? Does the collapse of faith in line-drawing imply the impossibility of limited government? Perhaps not. This chapter presents a study of an emergent, alternative strategy for limiting government, one that is fast gaining momentum among political and legal theorists friendly to the liberal project but critical of the line-drawing approach. In recent years, a contingent of Anglo-American political philosophers and legal theorists has begun to lay the groundwork for a reconceptualization of limited government in liberal democratic societies. Taking as their starting point a recognition of pluralism as an irreducible condition in liberal societies, these thinkers urge a reorientation in liberal theorizing, away from the search for pre-political limiting principles and toward a consideration of how to design political institutions capable of mediating conflicts and generating compromises.[3] In the words of the political philosopher John Gray, this alternative approach rests on the view that "instead of seeing liberalism as a system of universal principles, we can think of it as the enterprise of pursuing terms of coexistence among different ways of life."[4] Or as Bellamy explains: "A genuinely pluralist liberalism must change from being a meta-political doctrine of liberal values to become a democratic politics of compromise."[5] For thinkers of this persuasion, the goal of liberal theorizing no longer is to identify core liberal principles, but rather to figure out how liberal citizens might live peaceably together in the absence of such agreements. The work of recent theorists suggests that a philosophical commitment to pluralist liberalism carries with it distinctive political and institutional implications. Pluralist liberals argue for a conception of rights which emphasizes the politically evolving rather than the fixed nature of rights in a liberal regime. Whereas it is typical for liberal theorists to assume that rights must be constitutionalized in order to be protected, pluralist liberals recognize the significance of political rights—that is, rights established in the legislative process rather than enshrined in a pre-political constitution.[6] Relatedly, pluralist liberals also typically advocate for a regime based on the principle of legislative supremacy, indicting judicial review as antidemocratic.[7]

In pointed contrast to thinkers like Hayek and Rawls, pluralist liberals forthrightly defend the proposition that the sphere of legislative politics is the appropriate place to stage debates about the nature of fundamental rights and the limits of political power.[8] To be convincing, however, pluralist liberals must demonstrate that political power can be effectively contained in a system in which fundamental questions of justice are resolved in the legislative sphere rather than presettled by resorting to liberal principles. Otherwise, pluralist liberalism appears to be nothing more than a prescription for legislative tyranny, tantamount to a concession of the impossibility of limited government. Legal and political theorist Jeremy Waldron has emerged as one of the leading voices in a campaign to shift the emphasis in liberal theory away from a focus on pre-political principles and toward an understanding of the political nature of rights, and in this chapter I explore his alternative vision of limited government. In two recent books, *The Dignity of Legislation* and *Law and Disagreement*, Waldron advances the view that in pluralistic societies marked by profound and irreducible disagreements, fundamental questions of justice should be dealt with in the legislature, not the judiciary. Waldron positions the legislature as the site for deliberation about fundamental questions of justice, rather than figuring the judiciary as the body which enforces predetermined limits against legislative encroachments on liberty. Absent presettlement, a commitment to limited government still requires the government to obey prevailing understandings of rights and limits, but Waldron's view emphasizes the importance of acknowledging that (a) these limits are subject to revision and change; and (b) that there is a fair political process for ongoing discussion about the deployment of power.[9] At the heart of Waldron's alternative vision of the liberal ideal lies the claim that a limited government is one in which the legislature conforms to fundamental principles of justice which are themselves the outcome of a legislative deliberation. Limited government cannot be a matter of the judicial enforcement of pre-settled principles, for Waldron believes that disagreement about principles of justice themselves is an irreducible "circumstance of politics." His is a vision of limited government, then, which focuses on the democratic control of government, rather than philosophical control of democracy. In Waldron's view, liberals should acknowledge that limits must be left open to political debate, given the constraints that liberal principles place on what the government can do are minimal. Liberal governments have an enormous amount of latitude, and it is up to the people who live in liberal societies to decide for themselves what they think the government should and should not be doing. These are proper legislative, not judicial questions, because, as Waldron explains, it is the legislature which best represents the diversity and complexity constitutive of the liberal polity. Suggesting that in a liberal democratic political culture such as the United States a fear of legislative tyranny has led to the veneration of judicial power as a necessary protection for individual liberties, Waldron defends "the dignity of legislation."

Although Waldron moves in a promising direction in drawing attention to the fundamental work with which liberal legislatures are charged, I now suggest that his plan for limiting government is in serious respects flawed. By framing his critique of liberalism in terms of a contest between the judiciary and the legislature, Waldron exaggerates the representative nature of legislative politics, while at the same time discouraging exploration of ways in which citizens can participate in the exercise of judicial power. In arguing that limited government in a liberal regime comes down to collective decision making about what liberal subjects want their government to do, it is important not to equate the legislative process with popular sovereignty, for in many ways legislative politics are insufficiently representative. Rather than idealizing legislative politics, pluralist liberals should think about ways to maximize citizen participation in public decision making regardless of the institutional venue.

Waldron's Limited Legislature

Waldron takes as his foil the view, standard among political theorists, that those concerned with limiting government's coercive powers should concentrate their efforts on constraining legislative power. For liberals in particular, the insistence on the need to limit government originates in a fear that the legislative process can all too easily be hijacked either by powerful minorities or popular majorities who show a disregard for the basic rights of those in the minority. In his recent writings, Waldron seeks to unseat the assumption, widely held in the United States, that judicial review is necessary for the protection of individual rights. From this perspective, the judicial sphere is viewed as the appropriate venue for deliberation about the meaning of fundamental principles of justice, precisely because judges are thought to be above the fray of everyday politics, buttressed from the pressures imposed in facing periodic election and accountability to constituents. In this familiar vision of institutional authority, the judiciary is accorded the final say on fundamental questions of justice as a strategy for containing the power of legislatures. Because the judiciary is peopled by elites who are sheltered from the sway of public will, the reasoning goes, judges are better positioned to make determinations about what justice requires, including what the appropriate scope of rights is, and hence where the limits of legislative power lie.

In portraying the legislature as the primary locus of the threat to individual liberty in a liberal democratic regime, many recent liberal thinkers, especially those writing in the United States, seem to take for granted the necessity for judicial review.[10] Rawls is typical in this regard. In *Political Liberalism*, Rawls explains that in the ideal liberal regime, political decisions derive from a deliberative process guided by what he calls "public reason," that is, "the reason of its citizens, of those sharing the status of equal citizenship. The subject of their reason is the good of the public: what the political conception of justice requires of society's basic structure of institutions, and of the purposes and ends they are to serve."[11] Given Rawls's asserted connection between citizens and public reason, it comes as something of a surprise that he goes on to say that in a constitutional regime with judicial review, it is not the legislature (the branch that is seemingly most closely connected to the will of the people) but instead the supreme court which should be regarded as "the exemplar of public reason."[12] Rawls explains that in his ideal liberal regime, "by applying public reason the court is to prevent [the higher law of the constitution] from being eroded by the legislation of transient majorities, or more likely, by organized and well-situated narrow interests skilled at getting their way."[13] This statement reflects Rawls's image of the judiciary as a realm of principled deliberation, in sharp contrast to the legislature, which he depicts as a flawed domain in which justice is always threatened by the overwhelming power of the will of a strong majority of the electorate.[14]

Importantly, although Rawls insists that the high court be regarded as the exemplar of public reason, he concedes that justice as fairness does not in and of itself provide the basis for preferring a constitutional order with judicial review over a system based on the principle of parliamentary supremacy with no bill of rights. He admits: "political liberalism as such . . . does not assert or deny any of these claims and so we need not discuss them."[15] But while Rawls seems satisfied that no explanation is necessary for his decision to proceed as if judicial review were the best practice, his summary judgment in favor of judicial review is disturbing, since it entails an obvious loss of sovereignty on the part of the people. As political theorist Joshua Cohen notes, "judicial review does impose a restriction on the scope of decisions governed by majority rule processes and for this reason imposes a restriction on the extent of political liberty. If majority rule processes can afford adequate protection of political and personal liberties, then justice recommends this political method of protection."[16] Cohen's point is that Rawls's first principle of justice, the equal liberty principle, in fact implies that parliamentary sovereignty is better suited in principle to a liberal regime, and so Rawls is obliged to make an empirical case to explain his endorsement of judicial review. But Rawls never provides one.

My point here is to draw attention to Rawls's seemingly automatic embrace of the idea of judicial review, an endorsement which rests on an assumed rather than a demonstrated case for the incompetence of the legislature. It is this sort of uncritically disparaging attitude toward legislative politics with which Waldron takes issue, thereby challenging the commonplace conception of the courts as a "forum of principle" and the legislative branch as a domain of power plays.[17] In *The Dignity of*

Legislation, Waldron launches an inquiry into the long-held assumption that legislative politics is a degraded realm of "deal-making, horse-trading, log-rolling, interest-pandering, and pork-barreling."[18] As familiar as this view may be, it should also be disturbing, Waldron contends, for it reflects a tendency to disrespect and thereby disempower the very branch of government that most directly embodies the cherished principle of self-rule.

Waldron attributes the denigration of legislative politics among liberals in particular to an imperative faced by liberal philosophers to justify the enormous powers they typically accord to the patently undemocratic judicial branch. In Waldron's estimation, "we paint legislation up in these lurid shades in order to lend credibility to the idea of judicial review."[19] Though Waldron's writing is highly academic, in this regard his argument has a deeply populist appeal in suggesting that the time has come for the people to take back their government from judicial elites. Waldron's challenge to the habitual exaltation of the judiciary taps into popular frustration in the United States with a legal system which has revealed itself to be as mired in politics as every other institution of government. Waldron's argument also resonates with public dismay at signs of increasing levels of litigiousness in U.S. society, a social condition that one commentator has aptly dubbed "jurismania."[20]

Waldron's challenge to the relative priority liberals accord to the judiciary over the legislature rests on a sense that in liberal democratic societies, an insistence upon the need to protect individual rights has eclipsed attention to the question of *how* decisions about what these rights are should be made. Waldron observes:

> There is something lost, from a democratic point of view, when an unelected and unaccountable individual or institution makes a binding decision about what democracy requires. . . . On the other hand, if an institution which is elected and accountable makes the wrong decision about what democracy requires, then although there is a loss to democracy in the substance of the decision, it is not silly for citizens to comfort themselves with the thought that at least

they made their *own* mistake about democracy rather than having someone else's mistake foisted upon them.[21]

But in order to convince people that democratic decision making is worth the risks—including the risk of making mistakes—Waldron must persuade us that there is more to be gained by handing decisions about justice over to legislatures than may be lost. This is not an easy case to make. After all, one important reason for deference to the judiciary when it comes to debating fundamental questions of justice is that the judicial branch is structured in such a way as to facilitate careful deliberation, whereas legislative decisions emerge from the crude calculus of vote counting in a majoritarian system. What we sacrifice in representativeness in handing over important decisions to judicial elites, the standard thinking goes, we gain in knowing that fundamental decisions about justice are in the hands of established experts who are sheltered from the often compromising influence of special interests.

Against this view, Waldron insists that legislative decision making has the singular merit of resting on "a principle of respect for each person in the processes by which we settle on a view to be adopted as *ours* even in the face of disagreement."[22] There is both a normative and a practical dimension to this claim. As a matter of principle, Waldron believes that the legislature is the body most appropriately charged with debating basic questions of justice, because it brings together representatives who best reflect society in all of its diversity. As a practical matter, Waldron places great faith in what Aristotle dubbed the "wisdom of the multitude," the notion that, as Waldron understands it, "a number of individuals may bring a diversity of perspectives to bear on the complex issues under consideration, and . . . they are capable of pooling these perspectives to come up with better decisions than any one of them could make on his own."[23] Waldron traces the idea of legislation by the assembly back to the ancient image of lawmaking as "a process that related a legislative proposal to the complexity and multiplicity of persons, regions, relations, and circumstances, with which the proposed law would have to deal."[24] In his view, then, "the basis of legal authority has to do with a process (formal or informal) that brings together the plural and disparate experiences and opinions of those who are going to have to live with the norm in question."[25]

Based on his contention that it is the legislature, rather than the judiciary, that is the appropriate venue for making decisions about fundamental questions of justice, Waldron goes on to make a case against the constitutionalization of rights and judicial review. Weighing in on the continuing controversy in the United Kingdom concerning the adoption of a written Bill of Rights, Waldron argues against this course, warning that passage of such a bill likely will lead to the impoverishment of political debate, as citizens will come to believe that decisions about important political questions no longer rest in the hands of the people.[26] Against both the idea of constitutionalized rights and judicial review, Waldron contends that neither is necessary in a society in which the notion of rights is deeply rooted in popular political culture.[27]

In arguing that conversations about justice are properly staged in the legislature rather than the judicial branch, Waldron challenges Rawls and other liberals who assume the importance of judicial review in a liberal regime. While Waldron's conceptualization of limited government represents a departure from the familiar way of thinking about the problem of excessive coercion, particularly in the U.S. context, Waldron emphasizes that his approach has origins in the liberal tradition, in particular, the writings of John Locke and John Stuart Mill.[28] Recall the discussion in the introductory chapter which briefly considered Locke's view of limited government, a conception that rests, as does Waldron's, on the principle of legislative supremacy.[29] In Locke's ideal regime, legislatures are deemed supreme but not omnipotent, for Locke insists that legislative representatives must conform to the dictates of natural law. At the same time, however, Locke insists that the legislature is the proper institutional venue for making decisions about what natural law requires. As Waldron explains, it is Locke's view that "if there are controversies among us about natural law, it is important that a representative assembly resolve them."[30] From a contemporary standpoint, Locke's plan for limited government seems fatally flawed, for it seems to rest on nothing more than trust that legislative representatives will act in good faith to protect the public interest, including individual rights and liberties. But Waldron finds the suggestion that the legislature can function as a site for deliberation about fundamental matters of justice to be both "powerful and appealing," for, as he explains, "the institution which comprises our representatives and the institution which resolves our ultimate differences in moral principle should be one and the same."[31] Waldron hopes to cultivate in modern day legislators a Lockean sensibility wherein representatives recognize themselves to be sometimes divided by disagreement, but know themselves always to be bound by a sense of "mutual responsibility."[32] And if this sounds hopelessly unrealistic, Waldron simply asks that we consider the alternative—handing over the power to make decisions about the most fundamental questions a society faces to "a nine man junta clad in black robes and surrounded by law clerks."[33]

In addition to Locke, Waldron cites the nineteenth-century English philosopher John Stuart Mill as an intellectual progenitor of his approach to limited government. Mill's well-known essay *On Liberty* (1859) established his place in the liberal canon as an ardent proponent of individual liberties. In that work, Mill insists that "the sole end . . . for which mankind are warranted, individually or collectively . . . in interfering with the liberty of action of any of their number, is self-protection." Waldron suggests that Mill's reputation as a staunch advocate of limited government has eclipsed attention to the means he proposes for defending liberties, which emphasizes political culture over constitutional or other forms of institutional restraint. In Mill's scheme, the fate of liberty depends on society's ability to sustain active public debate and disagreement about the meaning of liberties so as to forestall the kind of complacency that creates the conditions of possibility for oppression. Following Mill's contention that individual liberty will never be safe "unless the intelligent part of the public can be made to feel its value," Waldron contends that "if we are concerned about individual liberty, then, the first thing we should do is not call for a Bill of Rights to be enforced by a court, but develop among ourselves a culture of liberty in which the idea is appreciated and taken seriously among those who will be participating in major social and political decisions."[34]

Harkening back to his liberal forebearers may help soften the shock of Waldron's proposals to dispense with such taken-for-granted protections against excessive coercion as judicial review and the constitutionalization of rights, but there is no avoiding the conclusion that in Waldron's scheme, citizens trade the comforting guarantee of pre-politically derived, constitutionally enshrined rights for the right to participate in an ongoing conversation about the nature of rights. By way of offering reassurances about a view likely to inspire unease, Waldron suggests that "in our modern preoccupation with constitutional law, we tend to lose sight of the possibility that our rights might be upheld and natural law respected more by the prevalence of a spirit of liberty and respect among the people, than by formal declarations or other institutional arrangements."[35] In other words, the very fact that limited government is a popular political value itself helps to insure that limits will be defined and respected. And while Waldron does not deny that in the last instance there is a necessary trade-off to be made in honoring pluralism and providing guarantees, he nonetheless resists to the very end the idea that what we are dealing with is a choice between a regime of limits and one in which power is unbounded. He insists that:

> the idea of rights is the idea that there are limits on what we may do to each other, or demand from each other, for the sake of the common good. A political culture in which citizens and legislators share this idea but disagree about what the limits are is quite different from a political culture uncontaminated by the idea of limits, and I think we sell ourselves terribly short in our constitutional thinking if we say that the fact of disagreement means we might as well not have the idea of rights or limits at all.[36]

By the same token, of course, a political culture in which the "idea" of limits exists without agreement on where those limits lie poses a risk to liberty if the pervasiveness of the rhetoric of limits dulls citizens to the actual contingency of their rights. The discourse of limited government, popularly expressed in the language of rights, gestures toward a presettlement that does not exist, thereby obscuring the power that citizens have to reformulate those rights. Waldron's high-minded invocation of the power of a creating a culture of rights boils down to the suggestion that we should treat rights "as if" they exist and hope that these assertions becomes a self-fulfilling prophesy. But this is a risky strategy, one that perhaps vests too much faith in the power of complacency to discourage liberal subjects from exploiting the enormous room for legislative discretion Waldron defends.

The Ideology of the Separation of Powers

Waldron's central contention is that controversies over fundamental questions of justice are properly resolved in the legislative rather than the judicial sphere, an argument rooted in the claim that it is the legislature which best honors the irreducibility of conflict and the multiplicity of perspectives and interests in a liberal society. He insists further that legislative supremacy of the sort he avows is consistent with a commitment to limited government, because ultimately the people themselves can be trusted to make decisions regarding the fate of rights rather than handing these decisions over to judges. In this section, I contend that Waldron's argument rests on assumptions that inadvertently reinforce certain institutional stereotypes which may undermine the kind of civic culture Waldron deems so important. As I explain, Waldron's alternative to line-drawing rests on an embrace of what I call the ideology of separated powers—the familiar, idealized notion of the judiciary as the branch of elite, expert rule, and the legislature as a realm of participatory, representative politics. In the following paragraphs, I question this description of the branches by way of suggesting that Waldron may end up misleading citizens who wish to participate in deliberations about justice. In defending the capacity of legislators to handle fundamental questions of justice, Waldron ends up exaggerating the democratic nature of legislative politics while obscuring the potential for democratic participation in other realms of government, including the judicial sphere. If Waldron's ultimate aim is to promote a culture of public deliberation about fundamental questions of justice, a defense of legislative supremacy is inadequate, for it overlooks the need to politicize all of the branches. The question of whether the talk of justice belongs to the legislature or the judiciary is a dilemma of false alternatives, for in a democratic polity such conversations belong everywhere.

Before proceeding, it is worth remarking that the following discussion of the legislature/judiciary divide in Waldron's thought is offered in part as an effort to contribute a new dimension to ongoing scholarly debates over what is familiarly known as the law/politics divide. In the 1970s, scholars who identified with the Critical Legal Studies movement especially sought to reveal the ideological work accomplished in liberal society by the notion that law is a realm outside of—or rather, above—politics, removed from the corrupting influence of power and interest.[37] In the wake of this critique, many commentators now readily concede that the boundary between law and politics is impossible to draw with precision because politics so thoroughly permeates the legal realm. The following analysis suggests, however, that a commitment to the law/politics divide is resurfacing in a masked fashion, albeit with different assumptions about the nature and "dignity" of each realm, as liberal theorists turn their attention to institutional questions surrounding the role and functions of the legislature and the judiciary in the ideal liberal regime.

Waldron portrays the liberal legislature as, in the ideal, a body "that brings together the plural and disparate experiences and opinions of those who are going to have to live with the norm in question."[38] Immediately it bears remarking that this vision stands in stark contrast to both the theory and practice of legislative politics in the United States.[39] In designing the federal legislature, the U.S. founders aimed not to enable recognition of social diversity (as Waldron surely would have liked) but rather to use the fact of diversity as a means to blunt the power of the people.[40] In *Federalist 10*, James Madison characterizes the pluralism Waldron celebrates in terms of the problem of factionalism. Madison defines a faction as "a number of citizens, whether amounting to a majority or minority of the whole, who are united and actuated by some common impulse of passion, or of interest, adverse to the rights of other citizens, or to the permanent and aggregate interests of the community."[41] Madison regards diversity primarily as a threat to the common good, suggesting that difference creates the conditions of possibility for the tyranny of some over all. In *Federalist 10*, he details the logic behind the design of the federal government, which is structured as a "republic"—that is, "a government in which the scheme of representation takes place"—rather than a "pure democracy," precisely so as to cure the problem of factionalism.[42] Thus, rather than celebrating "the wisdom of the multitude," as Waldron does, Madison insists on the need "to refine and enlarge the public views, by passing them through the medium of a chosen body of citizens, whose wisdom may best discern the true interest of their country."[43] Whereas Waldron writes as if a representative legislature is one which seeks to give voice to the will of the people, it is clear that for Madison and his fellow founders, the device of representation is intended to thwart that will.

Because Waldron's characterization of the ideal liberal legislature diverges so radically from the design of the U.S. legislature, it is not surprising that the reality of legislative politics in the U.S. is a far cry from the robustly participatory vision Waldron presents. It is clear today that the U.S. Congress in particular has failed to live up even to its limited representational mandate, as the problem of factionalism dominates U.S. politics. In part, this failure is attributable to certain mistaken assumptions and miscalculations on the part of the original institutional architects. Perhaps most fundamentally, the founders did not foresee the phenomenon of massive nonparticipation in the political process. Madison's scheme for the containment of factions depends on an equilibrium being created by the clash of competing interests. But if significant sectors of the population fail to direct the actions of their representatives through voting and other means of participation, the priorities of those in the minority who do pay attention easily prevail.

While Waldron may be overly optimistic about the potential for truly representative legislative politics, he overlooks significant opportunities for citizen involvement in the judicial sphere. In the contemporary United States, many citizens' experience of the state takes place within the judicial sphere, from serving on jury duty to contesting parking violations to appearing in small claims court to engaging in divorce proceedings. It is telling that most U.S. citizens are far more likely within their lifetimes to encounter a judge than an elected representative. In part, this relatively easy access to the courts reflects a broader trend toward what some scholars have dubbed a democratization of the courts.[44]

Waldron not only downplays the extent of citizens' involvement in the judiciary in portraying it as an elite branch, but he also presents an inflated portrait of judicial power, suggesting that in the United States the courts have "final say" over controversial issues subject to legislative debate. Waldron characterizes judicial review as "a system of final decision by judges" and notes with some indignation that "when citizens or their representative disagree about what rights we have or what those rights entail, it seems something of an insult to say that this is not something they are to be permitted to sort out by majoritarian processes, but that the issue is to be assigned instead for final determination to a small group of judges."[45] But does judicial review give judges the right of "final determination?" Not really. In fact, in the United States there is a tremendous amount of back-and-forth negotiation between the judiciary and the legislature on matters of statutory interpretation.[46] Here, the case of reproductive rights provides a useful example. Although the United States Supreme Court issued a decisive ruling defending a woman's right to choose an abortion in 1973, in the years since the landmark *Roe v. Wade* decision, a host of state and federal regulations have significantly contributed to defining, and in many instances reducing, the right vindicated by the court. In the case of abortion, it is clear that the language of finality implied by the notion of separated powers and provision for judicial review is undermined by the underlying structure of checks and balances in the United States, which enables ongoing negotiation about fundamental questions of justice, and renders the promise of judicially fixed settlements a false pretense.

A related argument can be made in response to Waldron's suggestion that provision for judicial review means that the people are not "permitted" to resolve issues by majoritarian processes. Again, the abortion case presents a telling counterexample. With reference to the debate over reproductive rights in the United States, Waldron observes:

> My experience is that national debates about abortion are as robust and well-informed in countries like the United Kingdom and New Zealand, where they are not constitutionalized, as they are in the United States—the more so perhaps because they are uncontaminated by quibbling about how to interpret the text of an eighteenth century document. It is sometimes liberating to be able to discuss issues like abortion directly, on the principles that ought to be engaged, rather than having to scramble around constructing those principles out of the scraps of some sacred text, in a tendentious exercise in constitutional calligraphy.[47]

Waldron's implication that, outside the courts, debate about abortion in the United States is "constitutionalized" is unjustified. While it is true that activists on all sides of the debate have appropriated the discourse of rights to frame their campaigns, the rights in question are not those explicitly named in the U.S. Constitution, but rather competing public conceptions of fundamental rights, like "the right to life" or "autonomy rights."[48] Ironically, this kind of popular discourse about rights, staged outside of considerations of the terms of the constitutional text, would seem to be precisely what Waldron is calling for in advocating public debate about fundamental questions of justice including the meaning of core rights.

One further implication to be drawn from the abortion example concerns Waldron's assumption regarding the separability of legislative and judicial functions in the United States. Two examples illustrate this point. The first is the case of mandatory minimums in the realm of sentencing. The practice of legislative specification of mandatory minimum sentences for certain crimes rose to prominence in the United States in the 1980s as an aspect of then President Ronald Reagan's War on Drugs. In the 1990s, the issue again catapulted to national prominence following the passage of a tough "three-strikes" law in a statewide public referendum in the state of California. These legislative incursions onto traditionally judicial terrain aim to constrain the discretion judges historically have enjoyed in determining sentences for individuals convicted of a crime. Both the federal sentencing guidelines for drug crimes and California's three strikes law have evoked angry opposition from judges, who suggest that these laws constitute a violation of the principle of separated powers and hamstring the ability of the courts to check the political branches.

A second example of the way in which legislative and judicial powers are intermingled in the United States is illustrated in the case of jury nullification. Law professor Nancy King defines jury nullification as the process whereby "jurors in criminal cases occasionally 'nullify' the law by acquitting defendants whom they believe to be guilty according to the instructions given them in court."[49] Jurors may resort to nullification for a wide array of reasons, including the belief that the law itself is unjust. Jury nullification is a controversial practice for several reasons, but at the heart of the opposition to it is the idea that it affronts democracy by subverting the formal legislative process. Given that juries are not democratically accountable, opponents insist they should not be given the discretion to make law. On the other side of the debate are those who suggest that the jury system is one of the very few opportunities citizens have to directly participate in the political process. As well, proponents point out that citizens have shown great circumspection in using jury nullification, and that when it is used, nullification has spurred much needed legislative change.[50] In addition to challenging the pretense of a strict divide between judicial and legislative powers in the United States, the case of jury nullification brings to the fore the matter of just what is meant in giving voice to the people. While, due to their small size, no single jury can function as a representative of the will of the people, juries do afford citizens a rare opportunity to participate directly in the political process, in both a judicial capacity (rendering a judgment about innocence and guilt) and in a legislative capacity (in choosing whether or not to apply the law as stated).

What are the implications for Waldron's argument of deconstructing the legislature/judiciary divide in the way I have suggested? In exaggerating the representative nature of legislative politics, Waldron risks reinforcing precisely the kind of democracy disabling complacency he attributes to a society enthralled by judicial supremacy. While it may be the case that historically liberals have unfairly disparaged legislative politics, Waldron risks a dangerous form of overcompensation in encouraging citizens to equate legislative politics as we know it with the robust form of pluralist deliberation he envisions as the liberal ideal. In seeking to dignify the legislature on grounds that idealize an inherently flawed institution, Waldron undercuts the development of the very sort of civic culture that lies at the heart of his own prescription for limited government.

Beyond the Legislature/Judiciary Divide

Recent defenders of legislative politics like Waldron sometimes make it sound as if judicial review has enabled the judiciary to hijack the political process, stealing from the people the right to deliberate about the fundamental principles of justice guiding and constraining the deployment of political power. The suggestion that somehow the judiciary has arrogated democratic power, however, is at best a partial explanation for the anemic state of political participation in the contemporary United States—an issue which I discuss in the next chapter. The encroachment of the courts into the domain of politics is at least in part the effect of a widespread popular and official abdication of legislative responsibilities. At its origins, the United States' political system was designed as a grand tug-of-war, a struggle fought among the various branches of government and between the people and their representatives. The inflated role played by the courts fills a vacuum left by legislators and the public, who in many cases have demonstrated an eagerness to submit society's most vexing political questions for judicial resolution.

Whereas from a democratic standpoint, it is easy to depict the courts as aggrandizing usurpers of political power, from a liberal citizen's perspective, the courts make a valuable contribution in liberating the citizenry from the burdens of political decision making so that individuals can go about the business of leading their own lives. Of course, in order for this arrangement to seem legitimate, the public must come to regard the work of the courts as serving the goal not just of expediency, but of justice— and it is perhaps for this reason that the courts (popularly emblematized by the Supreme Court) maintain a position of almost sacred regard in the United States. It has been widely remarked that the United States is a nation enthralled by law, hardly the disposition one would expect in a nation that takes such pride in its founding commitment to popular sovereignty. While in their rhetoric U.S. citizens may foreground their commitment to representative government over an equally ingrained and entrenched willingness to accept judicial settlements, in practice Americans are stalwart defenders of the courts, seeking to be spared the turbulence and instability of everyday politics.

Hoping to shake the public from its passive reliance on the judiciary to guard individual rights and establish limits on legislative power, Waldron offers a normative argument in defense of the "dignity" of legislative politics. He seeks to lend an aura of respectability to the long disparaged enterprise of legislative decision making, with the hope that higher public esteem for legislative politics will lead to a higher quality of legislative deliberation about the issues that matter most to liberal citizens. But given the limitations of legislative politics in a large-scale, representative regime, perhaps what is needed is not so much a normative case for legislatures as a practical one. In the previous chapters, I have suggested that despite the pretense of line-drawing, in a liberal society fundamental questions of rights and limits are left open to debate in the political process. If this is the case, then the urgent point for liberal subjects is not that participation in legislative politics is a noble undertaking, but rather that it is necessary to the extent that they want to participate in determining where the limits of power lie. Rather than dethroning the judiciary and dignifying the legislature, as Waldron seeks to do, liberal subjects should be encouraged to give up on the idea that any single branch of government can ever fully be trusted to express their will, and instead turn their attention to creating multiple outlets for political expression, negotiation, and contestation, always in the recognition that there is no single institution capable of fully reflecting the diversity of the popular will. This is the topic to which I turn in the final two chapters. As I argue, as the boundaries between politics and culture blur, it is increasingly necessary for political theorists to look beyond the realm of official politics and into the domain of popular political culture as they seek new ways to foster the politicization of power.

C H A P T E R   F I V E

Liberalism in the Age of Reality TV

Given the incompatibility of line-drawing as a strategy for limiting government with liberalism's core commitments, it is welcome to see a growing interest in alternative approaches among political theorists sympathetic to the project of liberal democracy. In the last chapter, I explored one such approach proposed by Jeremy Waldron. Waldron argues for "the dignity of legislation," contending that for too long liberals have denied the fundamental work that takes place in the legislature, where a liberal polity comes together to make decisions about the legitimate scope and reach of political power. While a recognition of the impossibility of liberal line-drawing might lead to greater appreciation of the significance of legislative politics in a liberal regime, one must be careful not to venerate legislative politics, as Waldron does, at the expense of seriously engaging ongoing concerns about excessive coercion in a liberal regime. In the end, Waldron's institutional optimism about seating democracy in the legislative branch may contribute to the very kind of complacency that enables oppression in the first place.

If the problem with Waldron's conception of the ideal liberal regime is that he ignores the potential for legislative tyranny, perhaps the corrective approach lies in adopting a more expansive conception of what it means to politicize the democratic process in a liberal regime. In this regard, it is worth taking a closer look at the recent writings of another contemporary political theorist, Richard Bellamy. Like Waldron, Bellamy advocates for a political as opposed to a philosophical approach to determining where the constraints on legislative power lie. Specifically, Bellamy contends that the ideal of liberal democracy should yield to what he calls democratic liberalism. As Bellamy explains, "the key to this democratic liberalism lies in institutional mechanisms that disperse power amongst the appropriate mix of actors to ensure collective decisions respond to the interests and values of those they affect."[1] In a more practical vein, Bellamy elaborates that "whereas liberal democrats favour bills of rights and the separation of powers, democratic liberalism employs the dispersal of power to produce a social mix conducive to political negotiation."[2] Under democratic liberalism,

> justice becomes identified with the process of politics. Political mechanisms not only ensure all are subject to the laws and that no one can be judge in their own case—the traditional tasks of the separation of powers—but also that the laws connect with the understandings and activities of those to whom they are to apply— the side benefit of dispersing power so that more people have a say in its enactment.[3]

Bellamy's argument meets at least part of the objection raised to Waldron's approach, for Bellamy takes a much broader view of the kinds of institutional innovations necessary to enable democratic participation in the process of determining the limits on government. Nonetheless, Waldron and Bellamy share a fundamental point of convergence in that they both focus on *institutional* solutions as the appropriate response to the impossibility of line-drawing as an approach to limited government. That is, each contends that the proper institutional design can, in the words of Bellamy, "ensure" that the political process will generate consensual agreements, without having to invoke constraints grounded in pre-political agreements. But in emphasizing the importance of institutional reform, pluralist liberals like Waldron and Bellamy seem to shift the focus in liberal theory from getting pre-political principles right to getting institutions right. Reading the work of pluralist liberals, one gets the sense that these thinkers believe that if we could just settle on the best institutional design for democracy, then the risk of excessive coercion would be eliminated, replaced by a consensual decision-making process in which a plurality of voices are heard and reconciled in a peaceful and complete way.

This institutional optimism is an aspect of a more generally idealized portrait of democracy which lies at the core of visions like those advocated by Waldron and Bellamy. While highly critical of liberalism, both thinkers largely neglect to consider the complexities of the democratic ideal. However, in this chapter and the next, I contend that for liberals concerned with the problem of containing governmental coercion, what is needed is not simply a demand for more democracy, but also a call for a deeper and more sustained critique of democracy—and not just democracy as we know it, but democracy even in its ideal form. While in previous chapters I have sought to show that liberalism needs democracy, in these last two chapters I emphasize that liberals must do more than embrace democracy if they are to address the problem of excessive coercion. Indeed, the very significance of the democratic movement in liberal theory suggests that liberals must engage more intensely with the complexities of democratic politics, rather than seeking simply to constrain democracy, as earlier liberals have done, or to promote it, as contemporary thinkers like Waldron and Bellamy seek to do.

In urging liberal theorists to adopt a more rigorously critical attitude toward the democratic ideal, the approach I advocate takes inspiration from Benjamin Barber's somewhat surprising insistence that liberals stand firm against their democratic critics. Though Barber is well-known as one of liberalism's most vociferous critics, he recognizes that liberalism has a crucial contribution to make in positioning itself in a "dialectical," if not overtly oppositional, relationship with democracy.[4] Taking Barber's insights to heart, the failure of line-drawing may be understood to imply not simply that decisions about the deployment of public power be made in the political process itself, but that, contrary to the roseate portrait of the democratic process fostered in accounts like Waldron's and Bellamy's, liberal subjects should simply trust the democratic process to produce just outcomes. In urging liberal theorists to turn their attention to a productive critique of democracy, the goal is not to undermine or disable democracy, but rather to create the conditions for an appreciation of the need for ongoing politicization in response to the impossibility of resolving once-and-for-all questions pertaining to the extent of fundamental rights in a liberal regime.

To this end, the focus of this chapter and the next shifts from a consideration of liberal theory to an exploration of contemporary political culture in the United States. By treating popular culture as a foundational site for the generation of prevailing ideas of democracy and rights, these chapters are meant to begin to fill a gap in the literature of liberalism, which has tended to focus somewhat myopically on debates about pre-political philosophical principles at the expense of attention to actual politics. Thus, whereas the earlier chapters can be understood as presenting a democratic critique of liberalism, in these last two chapters I write from the perspective of a liberal critique of democracy.[5] Taking popular political culture as my focus, these last two chapters highlight a significant methodological consequence entailed by a liberal renunciation of line-drawing. As political theorist Jodi Dean—a prominent voice in the movement to bring the priorities and interpretive techniques of cultural studies to bear on discussions in political theory—observes, one purpose of intersectional analysis at the juncture of theory and culture is to encourage scholars to think more broadly about "how the political is produced."[6] With these final chapters, I encourage liberals to broaden the prevailing discourse of analytic philosophy commonly adopted by liberal theorists engaged in the debate over pre-political limiting principles to include the voices of theorists writing at the intersection of political theory and cultural studies.[7] Cultural productions, rather than philosophical debates, must take center stage in a liberal theory that proceeds from a recognition of the irreducible stakes of political contest in a liberal regime.

The subject of this chapter is an unlikely one: the lowbrow world of reality TV programming. But as I explain, the analysis of reality TV programming presented below is offered as a point of entry for thinking about one essential aspect of democracy, the practice of voting. In the preceding pages I have made the case that in a liberal democracy, basic questions about the use and limits of public power must be left for resolution through the democratic political process. Voting lies at the heart of the modern democratic ideal, commonly understood to be the most important opportunity citizens have to participate in collective decision making about the deployment of public power. The centrality of voting in a liberal democracy invites critical inquiry into the meaning and merits of voting as a mode of political participation. In exploring the role that the device of voting plays on reality TV shows, and contrasting voting on TV with political voting, I seek to disclose some of the hidden dynamics of the vote, and to raise questions about the adequacy of a model of liberal democracy which places voting at its core. My analysis raises serious questions about the capacity of citizens to limit government in a liberal democracy if voting is the primary means through which they make their voices heard.

Do Americans Hate Voting?

In the United States today, there is perhaps no political truth more self-evident than that Americans hate voting. In recent years, voter turnout in popular elections has hovered around just fifty percent, an embarrassment in a country whose core self-understanding rests on a commitment to democratic self-governance.[8] And yet, if voting is "out" as a matter of political fashion, it is very much "in" when it comes to popular culture. Over the past few years, voting has become a central dramatic element on a variety of shows in the highly successful reality TV genre, including such programs as *Survivor, Big Brother, The Bachelor,* and *American Idol.*[9] These programs may be thought of as "voting dramas"—shows in which voting serves as the narrative engine, and the at-home viewer is figured, either directly or indirectly, as the ultimate chooser. Voting dramas, I suggest, present a valuable opportunity to grapple with some of the complexities underlying the familiar and seemingly uncontroversial proposition that voting is the defining act of citizenship in a liberal democracy.

Interestingly, although voting is widely presumed to be the quintessential form of political participation in a liberal democracy, when conceived as a cultural practice, the act of voting has suffered scholarly neglect. While empirically oriented political scientists have examined a wide array of factors contributing to voter preference and turnout, most seem hesitant even to pose questions not obviously amenable to measurement—questions such as the role that political culture plays in supporting the notion that voting is the fundamental citizenship act.[10] At the other end of the methodological spectrum, political theorists interested in democratic theory have generally ignored the subject of voting, instead emphasizing the importance of more deliberative modes of political participation like town meetings and grassroots organizing.

A foray into the world of reality TV is likely to strike some readers as an ill-considered means to deepen our understanding of a subject as important as the significance of voting as a contemporary citizenship practice. There can be no denying that reality TV shows come decked in all the trappings of triviality: unsophisticated plots, undistinguished protagonists, and unabashed appeals to viewers' baser instincts. For many, the popular success of reality TV stands as a testament to nothing more than its lowest common denominator appeal, seducing the masses by flaunting conventions of good taste, all the while bolstering viewers' feelings of social superiority by parading other people's flaws. Not unsympathetic to this view, at the outset I wish to stress that in regarding the voting drama as a site for thinking about political participation, it is not my aim to dignify or redeem reality TV by way of an association with the more venerable realm of democratic politics. Nor will I follow the lead of certain eminent cultural studies scholars who have sought to highlight the important ways in which lowbrow culture can function as an empowering site of agency and deliberation.[11] And finally, in comparing voting on reality TV shows to voting in elections, I will not suggest that the political sphere should emulate the popular, for there is much about voting dramas—and the fact of their popularity—that is deeply troubling, including (but hardly limited to) the celebration of venality and superficiality that has become the very hallmark of the genre.

Rather than argue that the pop cultural realm is somehow an exemplary, ameliorative, or transformational site for political expression, I proceed from an opposing claim, that it is the very profanity of the pop cultural realm which enables it to function as a social space for acting out (though not necessarily working through) some of the constitutive dilemmas of democratic subjectivity—dilemmas ordinarily repressed in the public discourse of official politics. In U.S. political culture, voting has the status of a sacred act, and the authority of the people's will is treated as axiomatic. Against this background, questioning the value of voting or the merits of popular sovereignty threatens one's basic credibility as a voice in political debate.[12] Interestingly, however, nearly the opposite is true when it comes to discussions of voting in popular culture. Here, it seems more likely that a scholar will be regarded as suspect if one is *not* critical of the ordinary people featured on reality TV shows—and the audiences who love them. Treating the pop cultural venue as a kind of shadow realm in which anxieties and tensions produced by democratic politics are given free play and expression, this chapter considers some of the constitutive tensions and ambivalences surrounding the idea of voting as an ideal of democratic participation. These dilemmas bring into relief the ongoing relevance of the discourse of limited government in a liberal democratic regime, for the limitations of voting as a collective decision-making procedure mean that decisions about the deployment of political power must be subjected to ongoing examination.

Building in particular on recent work by socio-legal scholars concerned with the role that pop culture plays in shaping "legal consciousness" in the United States, the following discussion proceeds from the claim that the political consciousness of democratic citizens is organized in part around an uncritical embrace of voting as fundamental to the practice of democratic citizenship.[13] While bringing some key insights from legal studies to bear on the analysis of democratic politics, however, I aim to push beyond the contours of the familiar debates among those legal studies scholars who see pop culture as a threat to the legitimacy of the law (and by extension, to the political process more broadly conceived), and those who defend pop culture's subversive potential. In his recent book, *When Law Goes Pop*, law professor Richard Sherwin asks "what happens when law becomes just like film and TV . . . when fact and fiction grow so confused that a trial comes to be seen as just another show and law is just another construct?"[14] Sherwin's prediction is grim: in undermining law's autonomy, popular culture corrodes law's legitimacy. The logic behind Sherwin's blurring-of-the-boundaries thesis can be readily applied to the voting drama, where the pressing issue would seem to be the potential for the association with reality TV to cheapen voting as a core citizenship practice. Is the voting drama contributing to a culture in which television-viewing citizens regard a presidential election with the same degree of gravity and interest they bring to the choice of this year's Miss America?[15] Do voting dramas reinforce the view that the act of voting is nothing more than the expression of a personal preference, as opposed to an exercise in public spiritedness oriented to the common good? Rather than contend that the voting drama degrades political voting, however, I suggest that the voting drama helps to shore up the legitimacy of official politics by popularizing voting precisely at a time when voting as a political practice is in a profound state of crisis. And whereas many legal scholars worry about the potential of pop culture to undermine the law, those with closer ties to the field of cultural studies have been more likely to regard pop culture's subversive potential as productive. As cultural theorist Rosemary Coombe observes, "it is now critical orthodoxy in cultural studies that mass-media imagery provides symbolic resources . . . that may challenge social exclusions, assert historically specific trajectories, and comment on social inequalities." Again, while my analysis is obviously indebted to the approach pioneered by cultural studies scholars, my emphasis is placed on the ways the device of voting on reality TV programs reinforces rather than undermines the status quo.

In the next two sections I develop the suggestion that there are significant continuities between political voting and pop cultural voting, and that these continuities make it possible to view the voting drama as a realm of displacement enabling the expression of anxieties about democratic governance which ordinarily are silenced in political discourse. The world depicted on reality TV shows bears enough of a resemblance to what is commonly referred to as reality to resonate with the experience of viewers, but it is artificial enough to encourage the free expression of ideas that would be viewed as heretical if delivered as political commentary. The voting drama may be viewed productively as a place where paradoxes of democracy generally, and voting in particular, are played out. At the same time, while it is illuminating to conceive of reality TV as a parallel political universe, it is also important to recognize the many differences distinguishing the realm of official politics from reality TV. Following a closer consideration of some of these contrasts, I conclude with a consideration of the future of reality TV and its bearing on discourses of limited government.

One final preliminary note: the observations which follow come at a time of increasing anxiety in the United States about the collapse of the distinction between the realms of politics and entertainment. The well-publicized California recall election of 2003 which resulted in sitting Governor Gray Davis being replaced by movie-star-turned-politician Arnold Schwarzenegger stirred a tidal wave of distressed commentary from observers who failed to see a substantial difference between a recall election which starred an action hero surrounded by a supporting cast of B-list celebrity gubernatorial contenders, and many of the offerings dotting the prime time line up.[16] The reaction to the California recall election sounded a familiar chord as only the latest episode to trigger concerns that the line between reality and reality TV has grown increasingly difficult to discern, and in this way, the kind of hand-wringing evoked by the election highlights an ontological inversion distinctive of our times: instead of the burden being on reality TV to defend its claim to be presenting reality, it is now the real world which must make the case for its distinction from entertainment programming if it is to maintain its flagging dignity. What lies beneath the anxiety about the blurring of the boundary between the sacred domain of official politics and the profane world of entertainment may be a fear that if there is no difference between these two realms, then all the criticisms elicited by reality TV apply to the real world as well, a recognition that begs a confrontation with the profound dysfunction of democracy in the present context.

Understanding Reality TV

"Reality TV" is an informal designation for a cluster of shows that first gained popularity in the 1990s.[17] Today, U.S. reality TV offerings are strongly influenced by European imports, including *Who Wants to Be a Millionaire* and *The Weakest Link* (both from Great Britain) and *Big Brother* (originally airing in Holland). Following the success of reality TV in the United States and Europe, derivative programs have sprung up around the world, including the first reality TV show in France, *Loft Story*, debuting in 2001; a South African version of *Big Brother*, premiering in the summer of 2003 and featuring residents from several African countries; and a planned dating-style reality TV show in India playing on that country's tradition of arranged marriage. Since early 2004, homes equipped for cable and satellite reception across Europe, India, the Middle East, and Africa have access to the 24-7 Reality TV network. Today, the reality TV label is being applied to a broad array of programs with varying formats, from game shows (*Who Wants to be A Millionaire, The Weakest Link*) to talent contests (*American Idol, Popstars*) to endurance tests (*Survivor, Fear Factor*) to elimination competitions (*The Bachelor, The Apprentice*) to domestic dramas (*Big Brother, The Osbournes*). While the term reality TV has become ubiquitous, its precise meaning is difficult to fix. The elasticity of the phrase can be attributed, at least in part, to an eagerness by entertainment industry executives to appropriate for new programs a moniker that seems virtually guaranteed to stir curiosity and thereby deliver big audiences. As a result, a show may be designated a reality program for a broad range of reasons including but not limited to a focus on real people (as opposed to celebrities) who are being real (as opposed to acting) in a drama that unfolds in the real world (as opposed to on a set or in a studio).

As the airwaves are increasingly dominated by reality TV programming, the trend has been likened to an invasion. But as film and television critic

James Friedman observers, "although 'reality-based' TV has attracted a great deal of attention in the new millennium, it by no means represents a sudden shift in the programmatic landscape."[18] In fact, reality TV borrows from a number of familiar genres, including news programming (unplanned events reported on location), sports broadcasting (unscripted outcomes), and documentary style, man-on-the street shows (originating in 1948 with *Candid Camera*, and eventually spawning progeny as diverse as *Cops* and *America's Funniest Home Videos*). Despite the name, reality TV also has roots in fictionalized genres as well, most importantly the soap opera.

In seeking to understand the emergence of reality TV as a full-fledged genre of its own, special attention is due to one pivotal forerunner in particular, the daytime talk show in the style of *Ricki Lake*, *Jenny Jones*, and *Jerry Springer*. Gaining popularity in the late 1980s, this emergent programming genre turned heads by unapologetically showcasing what were presented as "real people"—those not-ready-for-prime-time personalities whose very unfitness for celebrity status served as an entrée to national television exposure. Although the typical guests on daytime talk shows were plucked from the ranks of ordinary anonymity, many of the featured guests weren't exactly normal, and the daytime talk show world quickly came to be viewed not as a showcase for everyday Americans but rather as a postmodern carnival of deviance.[19] Nevertheless, the daytime talk show demonstrated that otherwise undistinguished people doing their thing could be every bit as entertaining as shows based on scripted antics performed by professional actors. By the 1990s, the notion of the real-time soap opera was in full bloom. Emblematic of the era was the show *Cops*, which married the domestic mise-en-scène of the soap opera with the rough-and-tumble world of police work. Robbing the domestic of its tranquility, *Cops* was a breakthrough in terms of breaking down the gender barrier by bringing the masculinized world of law-and-order into play with the feminized domain of the home. During the 1990s, other related developments contributing momentum to the reality TV craze included the OJ Simpson trial, which blended aspects of the male dominated world of news and sports with a story line rich in talk of romance, betrayal, and domestic intrigue. And then there was the Clinton/Lewinsky sex scandal, surely the apotheosis of the decade's intermixing of the real world of news with an over-the-top (and below the belt) soap operatic sensibility.

Viewed as yet another stage in the evolution of the real-time soap opera, today's reality TV programs place increasing pressure on the long-standing, if also long troubled, notion of a strict divide between the genres of fact and fiction.[20] On the one hand, reality TV seems to attract audiences precisely through its implicit offer of an intimate connection with ordinary people. Indeed, one suspects that for viewers frustrated by the increasing atomization and isolation of everyday life, the virtual access they have to the lives of the subjects of reality TV may be as real as a relationship gets. There is, however, a problem with this familiar explanation for the appeal of reality TV, for it ignores just how patently *unreal* the world presented on most of these programs is. The purported slice of life offered up on reality TV is not one that most viewers recognize as their own. After all, the preponderance of these shows take place in lavish or exotic settings, with plots driven by the nonstop emotional crises of exceptional people (whose distinctions can range from extreme wealth to strikingly good looks to a startling lack of intelligence.) Perhaps, then, in embracing reality TV, audiences are not grabbing so much at an experience of the real as conceding—and even reveling in—the conquest of reality by the unreal.[21] This alternate account of reality TV's appeal takes inspiration from philosopher Slavoj Zizek's provocative reflections on the popular reaction to 9/11.[22] Zizek takes issue with those who argue that the attacks were especially traumatic precisely because they pierced the unreality bubble, waking Americans from the numbing comfort of a collective fantasy of invulnerability. However, noting that many observers in fact likened the scene of the tragedy to a Hollywood movie, Zizek concludes that

we should therefore invert the standard reading according to which the WTC explosions were the intrusion of the Real which shattered our illusory Sphere: quite the reverse—it was before the WTC collapse that we lived in our reality, perceiving Third World horrors as something which was not actually part of our social reality, as something which existed (for us) as a spectral apparition on the (TV) screen—and what happened on September 11 was that this fantasmatic screen apparition entered our reality. It is not that reality entered our image: the image entered and shattered our reality (i.e. the symbolic coordinates which determine what we experience as reality).[23]

Following Zizek, then, we might say that it is precisely in the moment when life comes to imitate art that the idea of reality itself is finally vanquished.

How can we arbitrate the debate between those who view the rise of reality TV as evidence of a society grasping at the real, and those who see it as a celebration of the conquest of reality by fantasy? Does the "reality" in reality TV bespeak a yearning for authenticity, or rather a recognition that reality has become yet another entertaining fiction? At this juncture, I think it would be a mistake to seek to resolve this controversy, for it is precisely this ambiguity that defines the contemporary experience of reality. That is, ours is an era in which reality is conceived and constructed *not* as an absolute—as implied by the notion of fact/fiction binary—but rather as a matter of degree or a level of analysis. In this regard, it is interesting to consider the emergence of a para-genre of reality TV programming, what I'll call the "real-story-behind-reality-TV" show. As just one example, in spring 2003 ABC aired a one hour Barbara Walters exclusive with members of the Osbourne family, who are themselves the subjects of a popular MTV reality show based on the domestic travails of Ozzy and his clan. Walters' special purported to give viewers the "real story" behind the Osbourne family, but, in doing so, the program thereby threw into question the reality of the reality TV show *The Osbournes* in the first place. Despite the self-deconstructing implications of Walters' move, it has now become standard practice at the conclusion of series such as *The Bachelor* or *Joe Millionaire* to air a retrospective featuring rejected contestants who are invited back to talk about what it is "really" like to live on a reality TV set. In this endless regress, reality TV stakes its claim on the vast, unstable terrain between fact and fiction, defying the notion that a categorical distinction between these two realms can be established.

It is precisely reality TV's ambiguous footing in the space between fact and fiction which makes the voting drama such an interesting site for thinking about politics. The world presented in reality TV bears enough of a resemblance to what is commonly referred to as reality to encourage comparisons, but it is different enough to provide shelter for experiences and observations which might provoke ire if expressed directly as political commentary. In the remainder of this chapter, I argue that the voting drama be viewed as a place where ambivalences about democracy generally and voting in particular are given play under cover of the pretense of reality TV's insignificance.

Democratic Dilemmas

In this section, I suggest that the voting drama, modeled on the democratic political process, presents participants and viewers with some of the same conundrums confronting liberal democratic citizens. Here I identify three core democratic dilemmas—problems or predicaments facing the contemporary democratic subject—and I explain how they are represented on the voting drama. The first dilemma arises from the fact that voting is considered at once one of the most fundamental but among the least effectual citizenship acts. The second dilemma concerns the appropriateness of democracy as a mode of political decision making in a society in which citizens seem to love the idea of popular sovereignty but hate the common man. The final dilemma surrounds the role and legitimacy of a leader in a society based on a commitment to equality. Together, these dilemmas complicate our portrait of democracy, revealing constitutive ambivalences and even paradoxes at the heart of the ideal. In doing so, we are led to question the adequacy of voting as currently structured in the political process to serve as the primary means through which liberal subjects participate in decisions about the deployment of the coercive power of the state.

Before turning to a closer consideration of voting dramas, however, I want to pause to briefly explore the meaning of voting as a political matter. In popular political discourse, voting is most often discussed as if it is the sine qua non of democratic citizenship.[24] But why, one might wonder, is voting treated as more fundamental than other forms of political participation? Why is the non voter made vulnerable to charges of squandering civic rights, whereas those who fail to exercise other participatory rights, such as the right to speak or assemble, are generally spared accusations of civic dereliction? Why is voting considered an obligation, while other public-minded activities, like being informed, speaking out, canvassing, or organizing in-between election cycles, are treated merely as optional? In seeking to understand the status of voting as the essential citizenship practice, consider political theorist Jeffrey Isaac's observation that the equation of democratic citizenship with the exercise of suffrage rights is a distinctively twentieth-century phenomenon, one that emerged at a time when public faith in the appropriateness and feasibility of democracy in mass-scale modern societies faltered under the pressures of modernization.[25] Isaac contends that over the course of the twentieth century, the ideal of democratic citizenship was pared down to include virtually nothing beyond the right to vote. This downsizing of citizenship was undertaken to maintain the plausibility of an ancient ideal in the context of a social world populated by multiply committed subjects whose civic obligations compete with a host of other identifications and interests, for fear that if democracy were seen to require much of anything on the part of the citizenry, it would quickly be deemed obsolete. The veneration of voting then rests on a compromise with the ideal of democracy, in the sense that voting has been elevated above other forms of participation as a way to minimize the demands that citizenship is thought to place on democratic subjects.

Voting represents a compromise with the democratic ideal in another way as well, for voting is, in its very essence, a substitute for direct rule, and thus the vote is simultaneously a marker of the disempowerment, and not simply the empowerment, of the people. From a democratic standpoint, then, there is something profoundly perverse about the veneration of

the vote, where a loss of power somehow has become the highest symbol of the people's power.[26] Democratic subjects vote for representatives
precisely because they cannot rule themselves. However necessary a concession to practicality, the vote nonetheless is a powerful symbol of a loss
that has been ideologically repackaged as a privilege, a gift, a grant.
Acknowledging the limitations of the vote, however, need not lead one
to deny the fundamental importance of universal suffrage, nor to trivialize
the efforts of those who have labored throughout U.S. history to extend
voting rights to previously excluded groups. The long struggle for voting
rights in the United States organized under the banner of the motto
"one person, one vote" was and remains as much a struggle for equality
as it is an undertaking concerned with participatory rights.[27] One need
not dismiss the value of suffrage in challenging the assumption that
voting is the primary civic duty of a democratic citizen, for when the
vote is exalted over other forms of civic engagement—particularly those
that are potentially more disruptive or more potent—voting becomes a
means of pacification, not empowerment. Especially in the wake of the
2000 presidential election, U.S. voters now run the risk that by showing
up at the polls, they bolster a failing system, lending a patina of legitimacy
to an electoral process that sustains fundamental inequities among
citizens. Ironically, perhaps the most appropriate way to honor those who
have fought and died for the right to vote in the United States is not to
settle for suffrage, but rather to continue making demands for the real-
ization of the underlying principle of popular sovereignty, of which the
attainment of voting rights is but one aspect.

   In a polity in which it may be viewed as heretical to overtly question
the sanctity of voting, the voting drama challenges the solemnity shroud-
ing voting rights in several ways, by deploying the vote to make decisions
that are stunning in their triviality, and by exaggerating the ritualistic
nature of voting to the point of absurdity. In doing so, reality TV carries
with it the implicit suggestion that voting is not an intrinsically fair, just,
or dignified mode of decision making, but one whose meaning and value
depends on the social context in which it is deployed. The voting drama
mocks not just the notion of voting as a fair decision-making process,

however, but the underlying principle of popular sovereignty as well. To see this point, consider the fact that reality TV fans are often heard to describe themselves not merely as viewers but as addicts, couching admissions of interest in confessional, apologetic tones. While there can be no doubt that some viewers take a pleasure in reality TV that is entirely unself-reflexive, the over-the-top style of many reality TV shows encourages audiences to adopt a certain ironic detachment. In fact, reality TV appears to capitalize on what we might think of as the guilty pleasure principle: it is not the content of reality TV programs that titillates us so much as the knowledge that we shouldn't be watching such trashy programming in the first place. But in avowing our shameful love affair with reality TV, the claim to hate ourselves for loving to watch reality TV might just be a cover up, to mask how much we love to hate the people we're watching. In this way, reality TV becomes a staging ground for the play of a contradiction located at the very heart of the democratic ideal: loving popular sovereignty but hating the people. Reality TV enables viewers to revel in an anti-populist contempt for the common man without being held accountable for the political implications of such a stand. But what does it tell us about our commitment to democracy that we live in a society in which people spend several nights a week marveling at the stupidity of our brethren?

Voting dramas cast a jaundiced light on the ordinary people who comprise a democratic polity, but the genre also raises questions about those at the top. In a recent essay, political theorist Paul Apostolidis contends that cultural theorists have largely ignored the important subject of political leadership. Apostolidis argues that "cultural studies . . . persistently sidesteps basic issues regarding the purposes, methods, and justifications of political leadership," a scholarly omission which reflects, in his view, a broader tendency in liberal democracies to deny the significant role played by powerful individuals in putatively egalitarian contexts.[28] The issue of leadership is an inherently difficult one for democratic subjects, posing a fundamental challenge to the basic principles of equality and collective governance at the heart of the democratic ideal. Reality TV offers a promising field for exploring the ambivalent status of leadership in a democratic polity. Consider the show *American Idol*, which revolves around a contest between "real people" competing to become an ideal, where paradoxically, success implies that the winner is not so ordinary after all. On *American Idol*, the most successful contestants prove themselves exceptional in their lack of anything to take exception to— those who succeed are the ones who can perform Burt Bachrach songs from the 1970s one week while paying a heartfelt tribute to 1940s swing classics the next. The victors are the most agile parrots, not the most distinctive musical personalities, for personality is inevitably a liability in a showdown among aspiring pop chameleons. Watching the weekly winnowing process, one can only wonder: will the American Idol be the one who proves to be the most outstanding, or the least?[29] Of course, the same question lies at the heart of democratic leadership: is a leader one of us or better than us? In order to govern a democratic people, a leader simultaneously must appear to be both one of us and above us.[30] Thus, when George W. Bush was running for president in 2000, detractors thought it surely would damage his candidacy to point out the disingenuousness of a Yale-educated son of American political royalty playing the part of a naive Texas cowboy. But it is precisely Bush's double identity that sustains him as a politician, for his contradiction mirrors that of a people seeking a man of the people who stands out in the crowd.

The democratic dilemmas surveyed above suggest that the veneration of voting in U.S. political culture rests on a denial of some of the limitations and contradictions inherent in the practice. Taking these dilemmas into account leads one to question the adequacy of voting as a means for citizens to participate in the process of making decisions about the limits of state power. First, liberal subjects must wonder whether the provision for voting rights is enough to ensure citizen control of government. As I have argued earlier, the existence of voting rights may eclipse attention to the significant disempowerment of citizens in a mass-scale democracy, one which affords little opportunity for ordinary citizens to meaningfully participate in making decisions about how power is used. Second, the public's own generally low regard for the common man suggests that we may be ill-advised to rest responsibility for limiting government in the hands of the people, despite a principled commitment to democracy. Finally, democratic subjects must be careful to remember that even a popularly elected representative is still a potential tyrant, for once the public has spoken, the power of many transfers to a very few. Taken together, these considerations suggest the need for liberal democrats to rethink the place and structure of voting in a regime based on a commitment to limiting government.

Thinking Outside the (Ballot) Box

Earlier, I suggested that dilemmas central to the democratic experience are played out on the voting drama, and that by considering the voting drama as a site for the displacement of democratic anxieties, we may gain an insight into the repressed aspects of democratic subjectivity that bear importantly on the project of limited government. While there are important connections to be drawn between voting in politics and voting in pop culture, fundamental differences nonetheless remain. In this section, I highlight some of the ways in which the voting drama stands as a provocative counterpoint to political voting, and I argue that these differences challenge us to imagine alternative ways to structure voting as a political process in a liberal democracy. Though there may be widespread agreement that the electoral process in the United States is dysfunctional, efforts to reform the system will continue to meet resistance in a society which blindly assumes that an abstract commitment to voting entails an attachment to the particular set of procedures which have come to define the electoral system in the United States.[31]

Although voting is a central dramatic element in many reality TV shows, the viewer is most often involved in producing outcomes only indirectly, figured as a shadow participant for whom the thrill lies in watching other people vote—and then second-guessing their decisions.[32] Programs like *Survivor* and *The Bachelor* feature elaborate, end-of-the-show voting rituals in which the selection process is shrouded in over-wrought solemnity: flickering torch lights illuminating anxious faces, the long slow march to the ballot box, expressions of pain and regret as the inevitable elimination takes place. All the while, the audience follows along in living rooms across the land, second-guessing, cheering and jeering, fingers crossed that a personal favorite won't get the boot. Why do Americans love to watch other people vote? This cultural phenomenon might be read as a sign of the worsening of what I'll call the Beavis-and-Butthead complex—a distinctive form of social paralysis which first reached epidemic proportions in this country in the early 1990s among youths who no longer could be bothered to come up with original put-downs of lame music videos, preferring instead to watch two crudely drawn cartoon adolescents coming up with—what else?—put-downs of lame music videos. Today, one must wonder whether reality TV nurtures ever-greater degrees of viewer passivity by encouraging audiences to sit back, relax, and watch others engaging in the kind of decision-making behaviors that used to make it possible to talk with a straight face of active viewership.

Though many reality TV shows encourage spectatoring at the level of opinion-formation by positioning the audience as observers of a deliberative process, it is also the case that reality TV constructs an ideal of the voting process that is in ways far more active and engaged than the way voting is portrayed in standard news coverage of elections. Consider that many popular voting dramas feature private interviews with choosers, affording decision makers an opportunity to go on at length about the reasons and rationale behind their choices. Reality TV viewers, then, are not just watching people vote—they are watching people deliberate. And this feature of voting dramas stands in marked contrast to the way that political contests often are covered, where the emphasis is placed on *how* the public will vote, rather than *why* voters make the decisions they do. That is, in media coverage of the political process, the science of prediction predominates over the art of explanation, whereas precisely the opposite is true with the voting drama. The fact that deliberation, at least in the context of reality TV, has proved so engaging to watch suggests that more serious news programmers might take the risk in moving away from the horse race model of political coverage. It also suggests that the work of recent theorists of deliberative democracy, who suggest a host of political reforms from campaign finance reform to instituting a national "Deliberation Day," may not be as idealistic as it sometimes seems.[33]

Interestingly, one of the ways that deliberation is fostered on reality TV shows is by lifting the veil of secrecy that shrouds the vote in political elections. The culture of disclosure on reality TV shows stands in stark contrast to the anonymity of the voting booth, which Benjamin Barber memorably likens to the act of "using a public toilet: we wait in line with a crowd in order to relieve ourselves in solitude and in the privacy of our burden, pull a lever, and then, yielding to the next in line, go silently home."[34] In modern day democracies, of course, privacy in voting is regarded as a fundamental right that protects voter autonomy by preventing coercion or retaliation.[35] When the veil of secrecy is lifted, however, what ensues is fascinating. First and foremost, individuals become socially accountable for their votes, compelled to defend their decisions to a jury of their peers—and forced to suffer consequences if their explanations are deemed unsatisfying. Instead of treating the vote as an expression of personal preference, individual voters provide explanations in the hope of garnering the understanding and ideally, the respect, of other community members. In presenting a model of a culture of public justification, voting dramas invite us to consider ways in which the political voting regime might be altered. Anonymity in the voting booth may be a necessary precaution against abuse, but other sorts of reforms, both institutional and social, might be considered to accentuate the public-oriented aspect of voting. For example, while it is a common practice these days for individual voters to receive an "I voted" sticker as a reward for showing up at the polls, what about finding a way to similarly recognize those people who participate in registration drives, or provide services (childcare, transportation) to facilitate others who wish to vote? What about making election day a national holiday to encourage citizens to make the act of voting a leisurely activity which ensures time to fraternize with fellow voters at the polls?

Though the publicity of the vote on reality TV may encourage individuals to act with a greater concern for the common good, in other ways voting dramas reward self-interested behavior. For example, voting dramas like *Survivor* make the pool of voters one and the same as the pool of potential winners, so that by voting others off the island, the voter brings herself one step closer to becoming the winner. This structure encourages participants to use the vote to advance their own cause by voting against competitors. This feature of voting dramas stands in stark contrast to the situation in politics, where for virtually every individual voter in a mass-scale democracy, the burning question before each election is not "how will I best advance my interests?" but rather "why should I even bother to vote?" Considering the unlikelihood that any single ballot will make the decisive difference, coupled with a sense that there is little that ultimately distinguishes the major competing candidates, many voters fail to show up to the polls. Though it may be taken to unseemly extremes, it is sometimes refreshing to see voters on reality TV who are motivated by an active sense of a direct investment in the outcome. And one worries that profession of principled disdain for self-interested voting is used opportunistically to justify an electoral system in which individuals feel they have nothing at stake. While no one would wish to live in a polity in which individuals always privilege selfish interests over collective well-being, it is equally dispiriting to live in a society in which vast numbers of the public fail to recognize their own implication in political outcomes. In thinking about the kinds of reforms necessary to heighten public awareness of the stakes of political choices, several innovations are necessary, including altering the tenor of media reporting on elections to focus more on substance and less on personalities, as well as encouraging more thorough coverage of the policymaking process in between election cycles.

One final difference I wish to note between voting in politics and voting in popular culture is that in politics, citizens are asked to vote candidates *in* to office, whereas on many reality TV shows, participants are asked to vote people *off* the island, *off* the team, *off* the show. Of course, in recent years this distinction has been muddied in U.S. politics, as we witness the ascent of "lesser-of-two-evilism" style campaigning, where the strongest case made for a certain candidate is an argument against the election of someone presumed to be even worse. The popular interest in the California recall election epitomizes this trend, as the costly and time consuming election held in 2003 to determine whether to kick Governor Gray Davis out of office generated far more public interest than the election of 2002 in which he sought to be voted into office for another term. It is distressing to see the distinction collapse between a system in which voters are entitled to vote officials in versus a system in which voters vote officials out of office, for there are important differences between the two sorts of voting regimes. Most basically, a system conceived in the affirmative mode is compatible with the core ideal of representation, whereas the latter sort of regime reduces voting to an exercise in harm reduction. And relatedly, in a system in which voting out is prioritized over voting in, citizens are encouraged to vote strategically as opposed to expressively. Indeed, one function of the voting drama today may be to both legitimize and train viewers in the art of strategic voting.[36] What is lost in such a system, however, is the possibility that elected officials might actually represent in a meaningful way the policy preferences of those who put them into office in the first place. To move toward such a regime, it may be necessary to consider ways to diversify the roster of candidates so that a broader range of interests will be represented. In this regard, recent calls for reforms which facilitate third-party and independent candidates to run for office are especially relevant.

Into the Future

In the coming years, the boundary between political culture and popular culture is likely to grow increasingly blurry, as more and more reality TV shows take on an explicitly political cast. Among the more provocative and thought provoking new generation of reality TV shows is *American Candidate*, which premiered in August 2004 on the cable-access Showtime network.[37] Hosted by daytime talk show veteran Montel Williams, *American Candidate* placed ten contestants in a ten-week long competition to determine who among them "has the qualities to be the President of the United States." The winner received a $200,000 prize, as well as an opportunity to deliver a televised policy speech.[38] R. J. Cutler, *American*

Candidate's creator (and producer of the 1993 documentary *The War Room* about the Bill Clinton's 1992 presidential campaign) contends that with this show, "reality TV is returning to its natural home. Presidential politics is the Great Reality TV Platform."[39] Cutler's observation is tantalizing in its ambiguity: does he mean to suggest that presidential politics is nothing more than a game? Or perhaps that presidential politics, like reality TV, is, in its essence, an elaborately orchestrated show of authenticity? To be sure, *American Candidate's* blending of presidential politics and reality TV programming is disquieting, leading to the worry that actual political candidates might one day be plucked from the ranks of reality TV contestants, as the backers of *American Candidate* originally had hoped would be the case in 2004.[40] However, I have suggested that behind the concern that reality TV will have a degrading effect on democracy may lurk the even deeper fear that reality TV will reveal some of democracy's dirty little secrets—like the fact that the most qualified candidate sometimes fails to garner the most votes, or that the thrill of voting often lies more in the power to destroy than the power to elevate. Though critics and scholars alike seem convinced that the net effect of the popularization of reality TV will be a further erosion of the public culture of the United States, the public reception of the voting drama suggests otherwise. For if the past is any guide, it seems more likely that shows like *American Candidate* will reinforce, rather than destabilize, the political status quo in the United States. Crucially, shows like *American Candidate* provide a pseudo-political space which may help to defuse dissatisfaction with actual politics by creating an experience of participation as a substitute for political reforms. In this way, shows like *American Candidate* will function much the way that daytime court television shows in the post *The People's Court* era have. In the fictitious courtrooms of Judge Judy and her cohort of make-believe colleagues, plain talking mother figures dole out not tedious legalese but a homespun moral equivalent, and in so doing, provide a vital act of translation for a society saturated by law, making over the legal process into something accessible and legible to the masses. In a similar way, it is easy to imagine that

American Candidate will bolster the collective fantasy that anyone can be president, lending support to an ideal whose credibility might otherwise be threatened given the striking lack of diversity—demographically, ideologically, and otherwise—in the field of national political candidates. Rather than fretting that reality TV is lowering public standards of decency and diminishing respect for the political process, then, perhaps the more serious danger lies in reality TV's ability to prop up a democratic political system struggling to suppress confrontation with its internal contradictions and outright failures.

A program with perhaps more critical bite is *Gana la Verde* (Win the Green) which airs nightly on local Spanish-language stations in Los Angeles, San Diego, Houston, and Dallas.[41] Modeled loosely on NBC's hit show *Fear Factor*, each night contestants are asked to perform a variety of stunts that play on their phobias and fears—tasks ranging from swallowing 38 grams of tequila worms to jumping back-and-forth between two 18-wheelers as they speed down the freeway. But while the *Fear Factor* champion is awarded cash, those appearing on *Gana la Verde* compete for a different kind of prize: one year of free access to a team of immigration lawyers dedicated to establishing legal residency in the United States. Since *Gana la Verde*'s debut in the summer of 2004, it has consistently garnered audiences of over one million viewers per episode, and the show recently was ranked number two in its time slot among 18–49-year-old Latino viewers. Like *American Candidate, Gana la Verde* seems to bolster the legitimacy of the United States, most obviously by reinforcing the notion of the desirability of U.S. citizenship as a prize to be won at apparently at any cost. But *Gana la Verde* packs more subversive messages as well. On one level, the willingness of the show's contestants to publicly reveal their identities is a defiant and even mocking gesture which undermines the U.S. government's claim to be in control of its borders and capable of enforcing penalties against violators. As well, in turning the quest for a green card into a game in which contestants compete for access to legal resources, the show suggests that citizenship rights in the United States are doled out on the basis of privileges, rather than principles.

Certainly, the mere popularity of reality TV shows in no way assures that these programs will serve as an occasion for critical thinking about U.S. politics or democracy more generally. It is not suggested that reality TV shows are an inherently transformational genre, but only that they provide a resource for thinking about the limitations of democratic politics, one which liberal theorists might consider as they seek to better understand democratic decision making. In urging liberals to renounce the pretense of line-drawing and attend to neglected questions concerning the nature of politics, I have sought to suggest that analyses of the pop cultural realm provide a surprisingly fruitful vantage point for thinking about neglected questions concerning the limits and flaws of the democratic ideal. Especially for liberals committed to limited government, it is crucial to recognize not just the importance of democratic decision making, but also the complexity of operationalizing the principle of self-governance. I urge twenty-first-century liberals to turn their attention to the project of illuminating the strengths and weaknesses of the central institutions and practices of democracy, including voting, as part of a broader effort to raise awareness about the challenges facing citizens concerned with the threat of excessive coercion.

CHAPTER SIX

A Liberal Future for Privacy Doctrine?

Throughout this book, my central contention has been that liberal principles do not in and of themselves supply a sufficient basis for resolving the question of how much government is too much. Based on the indeterminacy of liberal principles, decisions about the appropriate scope and reach of legislative power cannot be resolved pre-politically, but must be determined from within the political process itself. For this reason, I urge liberals concerned with limiting government to shift their attention from irresolvable debates about the nature of liberalism's foundational principles to the question of how to provide for robust and inclusive public deliberations about justice within the democratic political process. Moving away from considerations of philosophical texts, this chapter and the preceding one take popular political culture as the subject of analysis, as I seek both to draw attention to the neglected aspects of the democratic decision-making process and to chart a course for future liberal theorizing about limited government.

During the 1990s, U.S. politics was galvanized by a popular crusade against "big government." Focusing on issues ranging from gun control to welfare reform, a movement coalesced around renewed calls for the containment of government. In the early years of the new millennium, the popular furor over "big government" has died down, but widespread public anxiety about the limits of the state's coercive power is still widely in evidence, most obviously recognizable in demands for greater respect for privacy rights.[1] This concluding chapter continues the exploration of political culture initiated in the previous one, turning now to a consideration of the evolving meanings and significance of the idea of privacy in the contemporary United States. In what follows I critically consider how liberal political theorists might orient themselves to recent efforts to establish the right to privacy as a core value in liberal democratic polities. The idea of privacy has long played a central role in the liberal discourse on limited government, in which line-drawing is understood in terms of creating a division between public power and private rights. Traditionally, liberals have insisted on the need for a strict parsing of social space along the public/private divide, demanding that this boundary be regarded as inviolable.[2] As law professor Anita Allen explains, "where restrained and obligated to advance interests in privacy and private choice, government is decent and tolerant in a way liberals believe moral justice demands."[3]

Those who welcome the current privacy revival owe a special debt to Judge Kenneth Starr, who has done more than perhaps any other single figure in recent American history to galvanize Americans in support of privacy—understood not just as a legal right, but as a cultural norm. Judge Starr's sprawling investigation of former President Clinton's role in the Whitewater land deal, which eventually led to an intensive inquiry into the President's intimate relationship with a young White House intern named Monica Lewinsky, sounded a blaring wake-up call to many in the public, igniting a torrent of concern about dwindling respect for personal liberty in the United States. Recalling the collective trauma of the McCarthy era, many were led to wonder: if Starr could do what he did to the President of the United States, who would be next? For others, the vagaries of the Starr probe revealed how little bite the legal right to privacy has in actual practice, a fact made apparent as Starr and his team of investigators sifted through Lewinsky's personal life and then stood idly by as tantalizing tidbits were unaccountably leaked to the public, eventually to be mounted on a Congressional website for all the world to see.[4] Beyond highlighting the impotence of existing legal protections for privacy, the Clinton/Lewinsky/Starr scandal also seemed to reawaken the public to the importance of privacy as a social norm.

In the midst of the scandal, many sought refuge in an effort to renew public commitments to seemingly antiquated public virtues like discretion and restraint. At the end of the scandal, privacy had been elevated to the status of a consensus value, widely recognized (if only in its breach) as essential for the maintenance of a civilized public sphere. And although the Clinton/Lewinsky/Starr scandal no longer dominates headlines, public concerns about threats to privacy show no signs of abating. Recent uproars over issues ranging from mandatory national ID cards to the protection of personal medical data attest to widespread public skittishness about imperiled privacy rights.[5] Especially following the 9/11 attacks, the pro-privacy movement has been newly galvanized in reaction to the passage of the USA Patriot Act, landmark legislation that removes longstanding privacy protections for citizens and noncitizens alike by dramatically extending the surveillance and investigative powers of the federal law enforcement agencies.

At the same time that the idea of privacy is enjoying a surge of attention in the political sphere, scholars are dedicating significant attention to questions surrounding the social, legal, and philosophical roots of privacy doctrine in the United States. The emphasis in much of the recent scholarly writing has been placed on re-describing privacy rights in a way consistent with underlying liberal commitments.[6] This reconstructive effort comes in response to an earlier wave of critical work emanating from a variety of perspectives, prominent among them feminist[7] and communitarian,[8] which were sharply critical of the role privacy doctrine has played in advancing patriarchal and capitalist agendas. In contrast to this earlier work, the new wave of scholarship emphasizes privacy doctrine's compatibility with more egalitarian social premises and more robust conceptions of autonomy.

In the following discussion, I hope to contribute to the current debates about privacy by considering both the capacities and limits of privacy doctrine to advance the cause of limited government. Without denying the enduring usefulness of asserting legal claims to privacy rights in certain contexts, I nonetheless sound a note of caution, warning liberals to resist calls to inscribe privacy as the centerpiece of their approach to limiting government. In subsequent sections of this chapter, I high-light some of the limitations of privacy doctrine. Next, I contend that the history of privacy rights in the United States demonstrates the failure of privacy doctrine to anchor guarantees against governmental coercion, for the judicial recognition of privacy rights has not reliably translated into assurances for many communities. Inconsistent levels of privacy protection afforded to U.S. citizens reflect the fact that prevailing social and cultural norms have established implicit limits on the kinds of behaviors and choices judges are willing to place under the protective aegis of privacy. Recognizing that in the past a right to privacy has been extended only selectively, I argue for a politicization of privacy doctrine. Regrettably, however, recent efforts to politicize the concept of privacy have been condemned as precisely the opposite by those who view the claim that "the personal is political" as tantamount to a renunciation of privacy rights. I contend, however, that there is no intrinsic need to choose between privacy rights and politicization. I proceed to argue that whatever the merits of privacy doctrine in theory, as a practical matter the public/private divide is losing relevance in a social world which renders such a boundary difficult, if not impossible, to maintain. Liberals committed to limited government, then, must look beyond the assertion of privacy rights if coercion is to be effectively constrained.

The Evolution of Privacy Doctrine in U.S. Law

The U.S. Constitution makes no explicit mention of a right to privacy. The closest the founding text comes to an explicit guarantee of privacy lies in the identification of the home as a place in which citizens are to be accorded special protection against governmental intrusions. The Third Amendment holds that "No Soldier shall, in time of peace be quartered in any house, without the consent of the owner . . ." and the Fourth Amendment states that "The right of the people to be secure in their persons, houses, papers, and effects, against unreasonable searches and seizures, shall not be violated." These Amendments attest in part to the fact that the home—materially and symbolically—served as a political battleground in prerevolutionary America, as the aggressive policies of seizure and appropriation undertaken by the British Crown politicized intimate spaces. In asserting the inviolability of the home, the founding generation sought to "affirm private property" and "attack the politics of confiscation," by marking the home, quite literally, as a threshold beyond which the government could not pass.[9]

For the U.S. founders the connection between privacy rights and property rights was an obvious one, and this is an association which survives to this day, reflected in public perceptions of who does (and does not) deserve protection from governmental incursions. In this regard, it is revealing to consider the flak that erupted during the Clinton presidency following revelations that the first family had successfully cultivated an elite cadre of "first hosts"—wealthy friends of the President willing to loan out their vacation homes for family getaways. At the time, a front page story in the *Los Angeles Times* reported in sober terms about the challenges the Secret Service faced in trying to guard "the first president in recent memory who has no place of his own to retreat to when he wants a break from official Washington."[10] But the real story came down to this: "Clinton has no real estate at all, not even a *pied-à-terre* in Arkansas. As a consequence, he and his family have turned first guests into a rent free term-of-art." Obliquely recalling the Lincoln Bedroom controversy—a brouhaha eventually eclipsed by the Starr probe—the *Los Angeles Times* report stands as a coy reminder that the Lewinsky matter was hardly the first time President Clinton had been accused of "sleeping around."[11] In a country notoriously squeamish about talk of social class, throughout his presidency Clinton's foes found it far more effective to indict his philandering than to mock his lowly origins directly, but the not-so-subtle tone of disrespect underlying the *Los Angeles Times* report is but one example of how easy it is to play on the slippage between disdain for those who sleep around for pleasure, and disapproval of those who do so for want of an alternative. Lacking real estate of his own, privacy was a privilege Clinton simply couldn't afford.

Although the ideas of privacy and property remain tethered to this day, the nature of the association has changed over time. One hundred years after the U.S. Constitution was ratified, the home had become a very different sort of battleground than it had been during the founding era, this time serving as a symbolic staging ground in a simmering class war. In the high Victorian era, privacy was understood as a hallmark of refinement, a marker of class status. Noting the "distinctly class-based character" of concerns with privacy at the end of the nineteenth century, legal scholar Randall Bezanson roots the emergence of modern privacy doctrine in a concern with "the 'problem' of access by the lower classes of society to information about the upper classes."[12] Interestingly, at a time in which status was equated with privacy, gossip in particular was viewed not merely as a personal vice, but as a threat to the social order, given its potential to break down the very barriers defining distinctions among classes. Against this background, it is easy to understand the crisis engendered by the marriage of the camera and the printing press during the late nineteenth century, a development that allowed for the first time the mass circulation of revealing images of the hitherto shrouded world of upper-class privilege. It was to put an end to these virtual invasions that Samuel Warren and Louis Brandeis penned their famous *Harvard Law Review* article entitled "The Right to Privacy." First published in 1890, this piece has been called "the most influential law review article ever written," and it is today widely regarded as the definitive articulation of privacy doctrine in American law. From a contemporary standpoint, however, it is surprising to discover that Warren and Brandeis' defense of privacy has little to do with an interest in protecting individual rights. Instead, the authors were far more concerned with the maintenance of social order and social hierarchy, goals that depended on the rigorous enforcement of a strict code of public morality. In their article, Warren and Brandeis denounce the press for crossing "the obvious bounds of propriety and decency," worrying that this development would "destroy at once robustness of thought and delicacy of feeling."[13] They continue: "No enthusiasm can flourish, no generous impulse can survive under its blighting influence."[14] Warning that "each crop of unseemly gossip, thus harvested, becomes the seed of more, and in direct proportion to its circulation, results in the lowering of social standards and of morality,"

Warren and Brandeis implore the courts to take a stand against the scourge of publicity.[15] Significantly, their case for limiting intimate exposures rests not on a principled commitment to autonomy nor a concern with personal dignity, but rather emanates from a desire to limit the kind of gossip mongering believed to destroy a social order that relies on privacy to maintain class distinctions.

From a contemporary standpoint, it is disconcerting to confront privacy doctrine's historical implication in the campaign to promote Victorian morality, since today proponents of the right to privacy often emphasize the role that privacy plays in preventing the legislation of morality. However, the civil libertarian conception of privacy doctrine is a relatively recent development, taking root in the 1960s when the legal conception of the right to privacy was enlarged by the courts to afford protection for certain sorts of controversial activities engaged in within the confines of the home. Despite privacy's presumed status as a fundamental right in the United States, the Supreme Court first gave explicit recognition to a constitutional right to privacy in its 1965 ruling *Griswold v. Connecticut*. This case arose from charges filed against the executive and medical directors of a local chapter of Planned Parenthood, both of whom were charged as accessories to a crime for providing information and dispensing contraceptives to a married couple, actions taken in violation of a Connecticut statute outlawing contraceptive use by any individual.[16] The Court found the Connecticut law unconstitutional, a violation of the constitutional right to marital privacy.[17] Declaring that "specific guarantees in the Bill of Rights have penumbras, formed by emanations from those guarantees that help give them life and substance," the Court went on to defend privacy protection in the context of the marriage relationship:

> We deal with a right to privacy older than the Bill of Rights—older than our political parties, older than our school system. Marriage is a coming together for better or for worse, hopefully enduring, and intimate to the degree of being sacred. It is an association that promotes a way of life, not causes; a harmony in living, not political faiths, a bilateral loyalty, not commercial or social projects. Yet it is

an association for as noble a purpose as any involved in our prior decisions.

Under any circumstances, such a declaration by high officials of a country which prides itself on a commitment to individual liberty would be alarming, but there is a special irony in the Court delivering such a statement in the course of a decision purporting to be a vindication of civil rights, resting as it does on a controversial conception of normative morality.

Inadvertently, then, the *Griswold* decision exposes the way in which privacy rights have been contoured by the courts to protect certain citizens, while exposing to public scrutiny others who challenge mainstream values. In 1986, the limits of *Griswold*'s conception of privacy were vividly exposed in the case of *Bowers v. Hardwick*. Here, the majority declared that the right to privacy does not imply that "homosexuals" have the right "to engage in acts of sodomy."[18] Returning to the *Griswold* precedent, the Court held that since there is "no connection" between homosexual sodomy and "family marriage or procreation," there is no privacy claim at issue in this case. In this way, the *Bowers* decision reveals that judicial recognition of privacy rights rests on a moral evaluation of the behavior privacy is supposed to shield.[19] The modern era of privacy jurisprudence in U.S. law suggests, then, a pernicious tautology at the core of the logic of privacy doctrine, for the law only exempts from public scrutiny those acts that have already been scrutinized—and deemed acceptable. In effect, the right to privacy reduces merely to the right to do whatever the law already says you can do. And so it is that the right to privacy affords no protection to individuals who, for example, wish to consume child pornography in their homes, or to those who would use controlled substances. In recent years, the ranks of the unprotected are growing, as privacy rights are being denied not just to those who engage in prohibited activities, but to those deemed members of suspect classes, such as immigrants[20] and high school students.[21]

In suggesting that privacy rights in the United States are limited by prevailing conceptions of normative morality, I wish to highlight the ease with which privacy doctrine, often portrayed as a crucial source of protection against governmental coercion, can be appropriated by the government as a way to advance a particular moral agenda. From the standpoint of those concerned with limited government, it is essential to see that official recognition of a privacy right does not in and of itself constrain the reach of official power. Privacy doctrine has the potential to promote governmental coercion as much as to limit it.

Privacy versus The Personal is Political

In earlier chapters, I have considered the challenge that a recognition of "the fact of pluralism" poses for liberals concerned with limiting government. Decisions about where to draw the line between public power and private rights rest on judgments about which rights are deemed fundamental, but these determinations inevitably privilege the perspectives of some in the polity over others. Thus, while one might expect all liberals to agree that it is important for society to recognize, and even constitutionally enshrine, a right to free speech, there is likely to be significant disagreement over the question of whether this right implies equal degrees of protection from governmental regulation for political, commercial, and obscene speech. But if the underlying purpose of limiting government is to prevent the use of governmental coercion to enforce controversial moral and political views, then line-drawing becomes counterproductive to the extent that it preempts further political debate about the specific meaning of rights. One implication to be drawn from this argument is that rather than defining a liberal society as one which entrenches rights, a liberal society might be better understood as one in which citizens are encouraged to challenge and critically engage prevailing conceptions of fundamental rights. A culture of debate about rights—rather than the pretense of settled rights—ultimately does more to honor liberalism's underlying commitment to limiting coercion. As I explain, however, in the case of the right to privacy, prominent efforts at politicization, especially those initiated by feminists, have been misconstrued as assaults against the very idea of privacy itself.

Begin by noting that the relationship between liberalism and feminism is longstanding, but uneasy. In the past several decades, feminist activists in the United States have been most visible in leading a campaign to protect reproductive choice, and the campaign has largely been framed in terms of a defense of the right to privacy. At the same time, however, feminist theorists and activists have vigorously contested the validity and merits of the public/private distinction so central in liberal theory, charging that while ignoring oppression in the private sphere, liberals have exaggerated the danger to liberty posed by public power. While liberals have historically emphasized the importance of limited government, many feminists have demanded greater governmental involvement in the everyday lives of citizens to correct pervasive inequalities. Advocates for gender equality continue to fight for increasing welfare benefits and the minimum wage, precisely because women are disproportionately represented amongst the most economically disadvantaged in this society. Further, feminists have demanded the extension of state power into the so-called private sphere to address problems like domestic violence and failure to pay child support. In this way, in the past few decades, feminist activists and their academic counterparts have been at the forefront in challenging the assumptions undergirding prominent liberal descriptions of the public/private distinction and legal definitions of privacy rights. Central to the feminist case has been the claim that historically the notion of privacy has served not to protect citizens from governmental encroachments on their liberty, but rather as a legitimizing shroud for oppression, particularly within the paradigmatically private space of the home.

As an antidote to the long history of treating issues such as the feminization of poverty and domestic violence as private matters outside the legitimate scope of public intervention, many feminists have rallied around the motto "the personal is political." The phrase itself first appeared in print in a tract published in 1969 by activist Carol Hanish, and "the personal is political" quickly came to define reality for a generation of women who saw themselves not simply as outsiders to power, but also as the effects of it. Political theorist Carole Pateman describes the message behind the slogan this way:

> "The personal is political" has drawn women's attention to the way in which we are encouraged to see social life in personal terms, as a matter of individual ability or luck in finding a decent man to marry or an appropriate place to live. Feminists have emphasized how personal circumstances are structured by public factors, by laws about rape and abortion, by the status of "wife," by policies on child-care and the allocation of welfare benefits and the sexual division of labour in the home and workplace. "Personal" problems can thus be solved only through political means and political action.[22]

In the years since the phrase "the personal is political" was first popularized, its meaning has suffered distortion at the hands of observers who have been quick to conclude that "the personal is political" stands in opposition to the idea of a right to privacy. This tendency was particularly pronounced following the Clinton/Lewinsky/Starr scandal, when public disgust with personal revelations reached a fever pitch. Writing in the *New Republic* during the waning days of the scandal, journalist Peter Beinart opined that "the personal is political" "has left American politics in shambles," and he implored feminists to begin taking steps down "the difficult road toward a movement that does not degrade politics by turning it into a synonym for life." Succinctly encapsulating the mood of the day, another commentator deemed "the personal is political" nothing less than a "powerful destroyer of private life."[23] To be sure, the Clinton/Lewinsky/Starr scandal hardly marked the first time that feminist champions of "the personal is political" had been charged with killing civility in the United States. Typical is the position adopted by political philosopher Jean Bethke Elshtain, who argues that with the popularization of "the personal is political,"

> what got asserted was an identity, a collapse of the one into the other. Nothing "personal" was exempt from political definition, direction, and manipulation—neither sexual intimacy, nor love, nor

parenting. A total collapse of public and private as central categories of explanation and evaluation followed. The private sphere fell under a thoroughgoing politicized definition. Everything was grist for a voracious public mill, nothing was exempt, there was nowhere to hide.[24]

Though it is the case that certain feminist critics advocate for a wholesale renunciation of privacy analysis on the grounds that the ideal is irredeemably mired in the patriarchal assumptions of the society from which it emanates, many, if not most, feminist activists and critics continue to embrace the idea of privacy, albeit subject to certain redescriptions and revisionings.[25] Rather than dismissing as hypocrites those feminist critics who simultaneously insist that "the personal is political" and demand a respect for privacy, one should recognize the compatibility of these claims. In asserting that "the personal is political," feminists seek to emphasize the fact that there is no domain of human relations outside the reach of power relations. In other words, when feminists say "the personal is political," they are challenging the traditional liberal conception of the private sphere as off-limits to state intervention. Insisting on the need to acknowledge that in some sense every aspect of life is the product of power is different, however, from holding that there can be no limits on government's right to regulate or coerce action. To say that "the personal is political" is to say only that private life is implicated in networks of power, leaving open the question of under what circumstances it is appropriate for the government to intervene. As an example, a feminist might declare that "the personal is political" as a way to highlight the fact that a woman's reproductive choices are always made within the context of a social world in which women are subject to discrimination and social subordination, but there is nothing about this recognition that is inconsistent with an argument in favor of preventing the government from restricting access to abortions. The right to privacy is best understood as a claim against the government, rather than as a totalizing theory about the proper exercise of state power. Commitment to the legal notion of a right to privacy in no way entails a denial of the pervasiveness of power in the private sphere. Once we understand that it refers to a limit on governmental regulation but does not imply the absence of power, the right to privacy becomes compatible with the underlying purpose of "the personal is political." The spirit of "the personal is political" lies in an acknowledgement of power without presuming to settle the question of what role the government will play in feminist struggles.

Feminism is committed to the politicization of power, and this is the spirit behind the slogan "the personal is political." But this meaning is lost on those who assume that a call for politicization is tantamount to a demand for governmental regulation. It is true that in politicizing the notion of privacy, feminists have called into question certain settled convictions about the limits of the appropriate reach of governmental power, in particular challenging the idea that family relations are beyond the purview of regulation. Thus, in recent decades, feminist theorists and activists have endorsed such public policies as provision for welfare and protection against domestic violence, policies which entail intimate state involvement in highly personal affairs. The important point to recognize, however, is that advocacy of such policies in no way implies the view that there should be no limits to the state's coercive powers, but only insists that these boundaries be drawn on grounds that honor the dignity and equality of all persons, rather than on an assumption of women's social subordination to men. In the end, the feminist critique of privacy reveals that in and of itself recognition of a right to privacy is not inherently progressive or liberatory, a lesson that is particularly significant for advocates of limited government, who may sometimes assume that the less government, the better.

Putting Privacy in its Place

Although the public/private distinction is strongly associated with the liberal tradition, the practice of dividing social space into two distinctive spheres of public and private long predates the birth of the liberal tradition. As Jeffrey Weintraub and Krishan Kumar observe: "Drawing lines between public and private—both practically and theoretically—has been a central preoccupation of Western thought since classical antiquity; and 'public' and 'private' have long served as key organizing categories in social and political analysis, in legal practice and jurisprudence, and in moral and political debates."[26] As venerable as the public/private distinction may be, however, today there is cause to question its continued relevance as a governing metaphor. Though privacy may be staging a comeback in popular discourse and scholarly circles, there are at the same time signs of potent countervailing social forces at play in U.S. political and popular culture which suggest that current paeans to privacy are masking more deeply rooted ambivalences. One need only contemplate the stunning success of reality TV programming in recent years, or the public's rush to trade privacy for security after 9/11, to doubt the depth of the popular commitment to privacy, despite vociferous protestations of offense when the public perceives its privacy rights to be stripped away too suddenly or too cavalierly.

In the early years of the new millennium, examples abound of cultural trends premised on a blatant disregard for privacy norms. In part, this reflects underlying changes in the nature and structure of social life in the United States, changes which might best be described in terms of a shift from a condition of familiarity to one of anonymity. As an example, consider the rapidity with which the background chatter of people on cell phones has billowed into a white noise tapestry blanketing the public sphere in many precincts of the United States. Significantly, the proliferation of cell phones signals the demise not just of the pay phone, but of the phone booth as well, leading one to wonder whether the social obsolescence of the phone booth is a cause, and not merely an effect, of the popularization of cell phones. From the contemporary vantage point, one now suspects that the purpose of the phone booth may never have been to shield passersby from the annoying strains of one-sided chatter, for it has become abundantly clear today that this public-minded consideration is not a high social priority. More likely, the purpose of the phone booth was to protect the caller's privacy, and this shield is no longer deemed necessary in a condition marked by anonymity, for who cares if you know my secrets if you don't know me? The social life of cell phones suggests that the very idea of privacy is premised on the possibility of being known, and conversely, that it is only in a confederacy of strangers that the kind of tell-all culture now thriving in the United States can be sustained. Put otherwise, shifts in the social terrain are rendering the idea of a private sphere obsolete, as anonymity displaces privacy as the contemporary subject's social shield. Though little may remain hidden from public view in a culture in which underwear has emerged as outerwear and web-linked cameras trained on bedrooms are increasingly common, nonetheless, ours is an age of isolation and opacity.

In this anonymous public sphere, there are not only signs that the public finds privacy unnecessary, but also undesirable. This is hardly surprising, for how could privacy maintain its appeal in a culture in which social worth is widely regarded as a function of exposure?[27] As an illustration, consider a popular porn website known as VoyeurDorm.[28] Launched in April 1998, VoyeurDorm is a highly successful X-rated site, indistinguishable in many respects from myriad other online pay-to-view porn destinations. Those who enter this virtual domain quickly find that Voyeur "Dorm" is something of a misnomer, for the scene is set in what appears to be more of a mansion or perhaps a sorority house, another one of those ubiquitous, postmodern communes first popularized on MTV's *The Real World*, and now a virtual cliché in mainstream reality TV shows. Home to a passel of 12 comely "coeds," VoyeurDorm is equipped with 55 strategically placed web-cams, all feeding live to the Internet.

At first glance, the principle behind VoyeurDorm's profitability seems obvious: VoyeurDorm offers thrills to viewers who get off, quite literally, on the violation of privacy—and what better way to induce the titillation of transgression than to stage a virtual peep show inside the sacred space of a "real" home? But taking the site's free virtual tour, it becomes clear that there is more to VoyeurDorm that first meets the eye. The tour includes a page featuring a photograph of each VoyeurDorm resident, and each snapshot is accompanied by a personal statement. In these statements, the residents share provocative tidbits about their sexual preferences and invite potential customers to have a closer look. For a site premised on the principle of voyeurism, these solicitations are clearly out of place, undermining as they do the voyeuristic pretense upon which the whole site is premised. Whatever happened to the guilty pleasure of stolen glances? One wonders: why isn't VoyeurDorm's fantasy-space structured around a violation of privacy rather than the performance of consent?

One might be tempted to dismiss this breach of pretense as a necessary concession made to the reality of selling sex in an inflated sexual economy, one in which being sexy means shedding not just one's clothes but one's inhibitions as well. And while there is certainly something to the idea that VoyeurDorm's "residents" are considered all the more compelling because of their unabashed enthusiasm for sex, I would suggest further that the site's contradictory setup caters to a public whose pleasure depends not just on transgressing privacy, but overcoming it. Consider that today's spectator no longer seems in pursuit of a glimpse of the kind of unselfconscious disclosure that once lured the voyeur to the peephole. Used in the classic sense, the term voyeur designates those seers who hope to find a way around the problem of what physicist's call observation effects—the fact that the very act of watching an event unfold alters its natural trajectory. When watched, most human beings feel impelled to perform, but what the voyeur craves is a glimpse of the real, a flash of authenticity. At the same time, many of today's voyeurs may recognize, at least intuitively, that sex—like gender, and other aspects of identity—is always a performance, even when no one is watching. And why go to the trouble of stealing glances when a good look is offered up for all who care to see?

Beyond the thrill of watching, customers who visit VoyeurDorm also may be paying to be desired. In a society in which subjectivity increasingly is defined by the act of spectatoring, wanting my gaze is tantamount to wanting me. In soliciting the customer's gaze, VoyeurDorm's denizens have the opportunity to act out the possibility of a *wanted* gaze, providing a clever antidote to mounting social anxieties about the growing pervasiveness of what law professor Jeffrey Rosen calls the "unwanted gaze"— the all-seeing regulatory eye of the government embodied in DNA databanks, streetcorner speeding cams, and the ascendance of "information-sharing" not just as a strategy but a social ethic guiding governmental efforts to combat everything from credit card fraud to terrorism.[29] Viewed in this light, the women of VoyeurDorm stand as powerful (role) models of the ideal subject of a surveillance society in enacting a love (rather than a fear) of being watched. As well, in eagerly inviting the anonymous gaze of the paying customer on the other side of a one-way camera, VoyeurDorm's residents lend a degree of respectability to voyeurism, shifting the peep from the realm of the shameful to the status of any other commercial transaction. While a society which venerates privacy regards the uninvited spectator as a pervert or a criminal, in the world of VoyeurDorm, the spectator becomes one whose gaze is solicited and enjoyed.

A final explanation for VoyeurDorm's renunciation of the pretense of privacy may lie in the fact that its customers want not only to be wanted, but also to be assured that the objects of their gaze are objectively desirable. If there were a time when Peeping Toms took delight in glimpsing the forbidden body, today the hidden body is more likely to raise suspicion, for if no one's looking, maybe it's because there's nothing there worth looking at! It's the same logical inversion U.S. youth culture has witnessed around the question of virginity; where once chastity was seen as a sign of good character, now abstinence is as likely to be read as evidence of undesirability. Far from cheapening its product, then, VoyeurDorm's motto—"Everyone's Watching!"—reassures potential customers that this is the place to be.

The point is that whatever the potential merits of privacy doctrine, the existence of pervasive social ambivalence about privacy means that efforts to restore privacy will constantly be undermined. The return to an ethic of privacy promises an escape from the hard work of making case-by-case decisions about the kinds of interventions government should and should not undertake, but I have sought to show that the easy route is closed. Instead, decisions about the appropriate scope and reach of political power require the public to weigh the interests in the sort of liberty privacy affords against the costs it entails in terms of connection with the broader community.

In emphasizing the shifting cultural valences of the idea of privacy in the popular political imagination of the United States, my aim in part has been to demonstrate to liberal theorists the importance of attending to the cultural life of rights when seeking to understand their meaning and limits. This task is especially urgent for those concerned with the protection of privacy rights. As discussed in earlier sections of this chapter, historically the concept of privacy has been closely tethered to social and cultural notions of the home, where the home is understood both in the literal sense of one's house as well as more metaphorically in the sense of domesticity.[30] The public/private distinction has been rallied as a defense of the fundamental principle, which still lies at the basis of privacy jurisprudence in the United States, that "a man's home is his castle." Indeed, one little remarked upon point of constancy in the history of privacy doctrine in the United States is the persistent tendency, as a matter of law, to project the abstract notion of privacy onto the home as the quintessential site for its expression. In his 1961 dissent in the *Poe v. Ullman* case Justice Harlan explained, "Certainly the safeguarding of the home does not follow merely from the sanctity of property rights. The home derives its pre-eminence as the seat of family life."[31] The preceding discussion of the development of privacy doctrine in the United States suggests that as the social significance of the home and "family life" has changed, so too have the ends and objectives promoted by privacy.

In the early years of the twenty-first century, the home has been conceived not so much as a refuge from the public sphere as an outpost of it, at the same time that the public sphere increasingly functions as a kind of "home away from home." What can be the meaning, then, of "public" and "private" now that a person can be both in and out, sitting at home but also out and about in the virtual shopping mall supported by the Internet? On the other hand, with the proliferation of portable devices like cell phones and pagers, it is also possible to be both out and in, for from the standpoint of callers at the other end of the line, someone is always expected to be home. In this context, the rhetoric of separate spheres and the broader liberal ontology based upon metaphors of realms, domains, and divides is losing its coherence, as it becomes possible to be all over the place without ever leaving the comfort of one's own home.

In the face of these shifts in social geography, significant scholarly attention now is being trained on the task of re-grounding the boundary between public and private. In redrawing the social map, observers on one side of the debate contend that the barrier dividing the private from the public must be radically fortified. Reading the triumph of the private sphere over the public in the victory of VCRs over movie theatres, chat rooms over coffee shops, and SUVs over subways, some critics warn about the dire consequences of a collapse of the public sphere at the hands of new technology, creating the conditions for radical forms of alienation and isolation. On the other side are those who insist that the dominant trend today is the increasing encroachment of the public sphere into the private, citing the virtual annexation of the late twentieth-century middle American home by corporate powers eager to reconfigure domestic space as just another portal to a 24-7 global marketplace.[32] Rather than trying to resolve the question of where exactly the boundary between public and private lies, I would suggest that the very fact that such a radical conflict could exist at the level of mere description attests to the incoherence of the public/private distinction itself in the contemporary context. This is not to deny that many experientially and politically meaningful differences still exist between, say, a public sphere that is virtual versus one that is physical, nor would I dispute the fact that an evening spent in an anonymous chat room differs in fundamental ways from the experience of an intimate dinner in the company of friends. To be sure, there is still much of value to be gained from further inquiry into the nature and character of private life and public space. Nonetheless, there are powerful indications today of a need to shift maps and to define new coordinates of social space as we seek to understand human experience in the contemporary setting.

My aim in this chapter has not been to suggest that liberals should abandon the concept of privacy altogether, nor to deny in all cases the strategic usefulness of invocations of a legal right to privacy. On a variety of fronts, from the campaign to protect reproductive rights to the effort to halt the expansion of state surveillance in the post 9/11 era, the notion of privacy has obvious legal and political potency. Nonetheless, for liberals it is important to resist the temptation to over-invest in privacy doctrine as the basis for challenges to the legitimacy of governmental interventions. As I have suggested earlier, judicial recognition of privacy rights for some has come at the cost of the denial of protection for others. At the same time, there is the risk that in mapping the social world onto the terrain of the public/private divide, liberals will distort and misapprehend social life, overlooking the complexity and ambivalences that mark the contemporary condition, and underestimating social resistance to privacy which ultimately may subvert efforts to reinforce privacy protections. Thus, although it may be tempting at this juncture in history for liberals to join the privacy revival and lend their voices to public demands for redrawing the clouded line between public and private, I urge a different course, one which moves beyond the false hopes sustained by the promise of inviolable privacy rights. The appeal of privacy doctrine lies in the comforting notion that there is some principle out there capable of resolving urgent social and political dilemmas of our day: how to balance values like autonomy and security, how to preserve intimacy in the age of publicity. In moving beyond the rhetoric of privacy, liberals relinquish the tantalizing promise of guarantees in favor of the difficult but interesting work of inventing new meanings for rights and generating new agreements regarding the deployment of political power.

The above reflections regarding public ambivalence about privacy suggest a fundamental flaw in the underlying logic of liberalism. Liberals have long assumed that the natural order of things is for governments to seek to encroach on liberty while individuals struggle to prevent interference. Liberal provisions for limited government emphasize the need to check official coercion, discounting the role that public culture plays as a mediating force in determining what rights people value and which encroachments register as oppressive. But if the recent privacy crisis in the United States has been precipitated not simply by examples of privacy

being *taken* away by governmental officials, but also by Americans' willingness and even eagerness to *give* their privacy away, then liberals may have
things exactly backwards.[33] If this is the case, we may have to take seriously
law professor Anita Allen's perhaps tongue-in-cheek and certainly para-
doxical suggestion that a respect for privacy must be "coerced" if it is to
survive at all as a societal value.[34] At the very least, liberal theorists would
be well-advised to direct more critical attention to the interaction between
political power and political culture. More specifically, liberals must think
about what lies beyond privacy, focusing on ways to convey an opposition
to coercion without valorizing individualism and inviting isolation.

Pushing Limits: Liberalism Beyond Line-Drawing

As liberals attend more to questions arising from a consideration of the
democratic political process, they will be led inevitably to engage
contemporary charges that democracy as we know it has failed, at times
miserably, to live up to its ideal. It may be tempting to simply join the
chorus of theorists celebrating the ideal of democracy, but what is called
for now is a revisioning of democracy rather than mere support. In this
regard, recent work in the area of deliberative democracy makes a
valuable contribution, as theorists increasingly are exploring the possibilities for new institutional arrangements to support democratic political
practice. Consider, for example, political theorists Bruce Ackerman and
James Fishkin's intriguing proposal for a new national holiday called
"Deliberation Day." As they explain:

> It will be held one week before major national elections. Registered
> voters will be called together in neighborhood meeting places, in
> small groups of 15, and larger groups of 500, to discuss the central
> issues raised by the campaign. Each deliberator will be paid $150 for
> the day's work of citizenship, on condition that he or she shows up
> at the polls the next week. All other work, except the most essential,
> will be prohibited by law.[35]

Political theorist Ethan Leib offers a similarly radical proposal for adding an official fourth branch of government:

> Composed of stratified random samples of 525 eligible—though not necessarily registered—voters, debating in groups of approximately fifteen, the popular branch would take the form of small civic juries occasionally meeting in plenary sessions to get their "charges." Such juries would debate political policies at assemblies convened for such purposes . . . Such juries would be called in circumstances where ballot initiatives and referendums are currently employed in the states that use them. In this paradigm, the popular branch would have the authority to enact law, while the legislative and executive branches would help with setting the agendas and tailoring the findings of the deliberative body into coherent written statutes.[36]

At first glance, ideas such as these may seem hopelessly idealistic and somewhat outlandish, properly viewed more as thought experiments than serious proposals for change. In contemporary U.S. politics, it is difficult to determine what, truly, is possible. Amidst a rhetoric of scarcity and a reality of ballooning deficits, the sky seems to be the limit when the goal is deemed important enough, as suggested by the case of the War on Terror. One wonders whether the goal of vitalizing the democratic political process will ever rank so high?

Whatever the practical prospects may be for implementing the kinds of reforms suggested by Ackerman and Fishkin on the one hand, and Leib on the other, merely as a thought experiment, their proposals are productive in bringing to the fore the value and importance in a democracy not simply of casting votes, but of participating in a thoughtful consideration of the issues. Taking seriously my contention that the ultimate check on power in a liberal democracy lies in the hands of those who control the political process, we are forced to confront the difficult question of whether the people can be trusted. There are many indications that democracy as it is currently practiced does not encourage reasoned, public-minded participation, a point that is too easily lost in an era in which we rarely strive to do more than simply "get out the vote." Instead of playing the role of cheerleaders for democracy, liberals have an important contribution to make in reminding us that power is not something that ever can be fully mastered, but always must be managed. While in the United States today it is undeniably the case that democracy is debilitated by low levels of citizen engagement, more participation is only part of the formula for reviving political society; there is much work to be done as well in educating citizens about the stakes of their decisions. For liberals committed to the limitation of power, these stakes include liberty itself, and in this regard it is important to remember that we are no more free for having chosen our chains.

Taken as a whole, the preceding chapters point a new direction for liberal theorizing, one which emphasizes politics over philosophy, particularity over principles. For those concerned with the question of how to limit governmental power, the argument in the preceding chapters is meant to be a hopeful, if not altogether reassuring, one. I have encouraged liberals to abandon the project of settling on pre-political limits and instead, turn their attention to the political process, broadly conceived, for it is here that decisions about the deployment of power are made. This argument will be cold comfort to those looking for fixed guarantees, but it is a call to arms to those willing to engage in the political fray.

NOTES

Chapter One   Limited Government
in the Liberal Tradition

1. President Clinton's State of the Union Address to Congress, January 23, 1996.
2. Lowi 1996.
3. See Wills 1999.
4. This discussion is based on the information provided in the *Oxford English Dictionary*.
5. Shklar 1989, 21.
6. Holmes 1995, 16.
7. Bellamy 1999, 1.
8. The significance of this tendency will be explored in greater detail in chapter five.
9. Kymlicka 1990, 251.
10. While the necessity of judicial review remains virtually unchallenged in the United States, the institution is not universally accepted in societies broadly conceived as liberal, most notably England. However, because the United States is regarded by many as the exemplary site for imagining liberal democracy, judicial review should not be dismissed merely as a national anomaly. As well, support for the institutionalization of judicial review has been gaining momentum in recent years in countries such as Canada, which authorized constitutional review in 1982, and England, which is currently experiencing a movement to constitutionalize a judicially enforceable Bill of Rights.
11. Waldron 1999a, 63–64. The following discussion is indebted to Waldron's argument in the chapter entitled "Locke's Legislature (and Rawls's)."
12. Locke, sect.135.
13. See the discussion in Waldron 1999a, 87.

14. See the discussion in Waldron 1999a, 83.
15. Kramnick 1987, 21.
16. Ibid., 22–23.
17. Rakove 1996, 307.
18. Wood 1969, 362.
19. Kramnick 1987, 25.
20. For more on this point, see Williams 2004.
21. James Madison, *The Federalist No. 10*, in Issac Kramnick 1987, 122.
22. James Madison, *The Federalist No. 48*, in Isaac Kramnick 1987, 309.
23. Jefferson to James Madison, March 15, 1789. Quoted from Rakove 1998, 166.
24. 5 US 137 (1803).
25. Notable exceptions include Tushnet 1999 and Waldron 1999b, both of whom issue sharp challenges to the practice of judicial review. Waldron's argument will be treated in greater detail in chapter four.
26. Barber 1997, 27.
27. Bellamy 1994, 419.
28. See Wainright 1994.
29. See Nozick 1989, ch. 25.
30. For an excellent introduction to leading libertarian thinkers of the twentieth century, see Newmann 1984.
31. Hayek 1976, 100.
32. Larmore 1996, 122.
33. Ibid., 151.
34. Ibid., 126.

Chapter Two   Liberalism Confronts the Welfare State

1. See Lowi 1979 for an excellent introduction to the issues posed by the emergence of the modern welfare state in the United States.
2. See Newmann 1984 for an insightful introduction to twentieth-century libertarian thought.
3. See Gamble 1996, 13–16 for a brief intellectual biography of Hayek. More in-depth accounts can be found in Caldwell 2003 and Ebenstein 2003. See also Kresge and Wenar 1994, a fascinating collection of autobiographical writings, letters, and interviews from throughout Hayek's life.
4. See Gamble 1996, 150–176.
5. In March 1945, the editors at *Readers Digest* magazine presented *The Road to Serfdom* as its condensed book of the month, an honor that carried with it an estimated circulation of several million copies. Shortly thereafter,

Hayek was invited to make guest appearances on a host of radio talk shows and at other public events across the United States.

6. Ackerman 1996, 214.

7. Barber 1988, 105.

8. Waldron 1993, 29.

9. Holmes 1995, 238. As this characterization suggests, Hayek is widely presumed to insist upon the radical curtailment of legislative powers, a depiction I challenge in the next few paragraphs.

10. See, e.g., Holmes 1995 and Sunstein 1996.

11. See Bellamy 1994 and 1999; Hamowy 1961; and Kukathas 1990.

12. See Scheuerman 1997 and Waldron 1999b. In *The Political Order of a Free People*, Hayek calls for "the containment of power and the dethronement of politics" (1979, ix).

13. Known for achieving a degree of public renown unusual for a scholar of any stripe, the Rolling Stones' Mick Jagger is also rumored to be among Hayek's fans.

14. Burchell et al. 1991.

15. Gordon 1991, 6. Gordon explains further that "Foucault was, one might say, sufficiently respectful of the historical effectiveness of liberalism as an art of government to doubt the liberal (and Marxist) nightmare of an ever-expansionist and despotic tendency within the state. Although not enamored of minimalist anarcho-liberal individualism in the manner of Robert Nozick, Foucault does seem to have been (at least initially) intrigued by the properties of liberalism as a form of knowledge calculated to limit power by persuading government of its own incapacity; by the notion of the rule of law as the architecture of a pluralists social space; and by the German neo-liberals' way of conceiving the social market as a game of freedom sustained by governmental artifice and invention" (47).

16. Quoted in Gordon 1991, 47.

17. Hayek 1944, 5.

18. Hayek 1960, 260.

19. Hayek 1976, 66–67.

20. Hayek 1979, 151.

21. Hayek 1960, 253–254.

22. Ibid., 259.

23. See Hayek 1976, 62–66. In *The Road to Serfdom*, Hayek makes it clear that he opposes not planning in general, but only central planning understood as the "direction of the whole economic system according to one unified plan." Hayek goes on to explain that "competition, on the other hand, means decentralized planning by many separate persons" (1944, 521).

24. Hayek 1979, 41.
25. Ibid., 44.
26. Ibid., 61.
27. Ibid., 62.
28. Hayek 1961, 28–29.
29. Hayek 1979, 11.
30. Ibid., 11–12.
31. Ibid., 154.
32. Hayek [1944] 1976.
33. Hayek 1960, 208.
34. Bellamy, e.g., suggests that "Hayek tries to avoid the charge of constructivism by stressing the formalism of the Kantian test of universalizability" (1999, 32).
35. As I explained in chapter one, line-drawing refers to a specific approach to limiting government which involves settling in advance of the political process precisely what kinds of policies the government may enact. In saying that Hayek does not draw lines, I do not mean to deny that Hayek seeks to impose limits on the reach of legislative power, but only that he adopts an approach to limiting government which does not rely on the kind of presettled constraints which specify what it is government may and may not do. As I discuss further, Hayek adopts an alternative approach, one which relies on formal and institutional constraints, an approach he favors precisely because it does not require him to name in advance the specific policies a liberal government may enact.
36. Hayek 1961.
37. Kukathas 1990, 157–158.
38. Hamowy 1961, 31.
39. Flathman 1994, 316.
40. Sunstein 1996, 118.
41. Bellamy 1999, 34.
42. Gamble 1996, 10.
43. Gray 1982, 51.
44. Hayek 1960, 209.
45. Ibid.
46. Hayek 1960, 154.
47. Ibid., 222.
48. Ibid.
49. Hayek 1960, 221.
50. Ibid.
51. See the discussion of Buchanan's critique in Gray 1984, 70–71.

52. Hayek 1960, 183–184.
53. Ibid., 138.
54. Ibid., 134.
55. Hayek 1979, 129.
56. Ibid., 128.
57. Ibid., 5.
58. Hayek 1960, 403.
59. Hayek 1979, 138.
60. Hayek 1960, 401.
61. Hayek 1979, 5.
62. Ibid., 38–40.
63. Ibid., 109. Note that although Hayek here establishes a clear limit on legislative power, he does not resort to line-drawing as defined in chapter one, that is, he does not specify the content of laws the legislature may (and may not) pass.
64. Hayek 1979, 113.
65. Ibid., 117.
66. Scheuerman 1997, 180.
67. Ibid., 179.
68. Ibid., 182.
69. Ibid.
70. Sheldon Wolin 1993 cautions against the pervasive assumption that "electoral democracy" is the only, or even a legitimate, form of democratic self-governance. The question of the relationship between voting and liberal democracy is taken up in greater detail in chapter six.
71. Hayek 1960, 222.
72. Hamowy 1982, 138.
73. Hayek 1979, 149.

Chapter Three   Liberalism and the Justice of Limits

1. Hayek 1976, xii.
2. Ibid., 69.
3. Ibid., xi.
4. Ibid., xi–xii.
5. Ibid., 70.
6. Ibid., 100.
7. Ibid., xiii.
8. Daniel Bell, quoted in Hayek 1976, 183.

9. Quoting from Rawls 1963, 102 in Hayek 1976, 100.
10. Rawls opposes redistribution when adopted as a post hoc strategy to correct for an allocation of resources determined to be unjust, but he does not oppose the idea of a basic structure which provides for redistribution.
11. Waldron 1993, 30.
12. Ibid.
13. Ibid.
14. Rawls 2001, 7–8.
15. Rawls's obituary, provided by Harvard University following his death on November 24, 2002 at the age of 81.
16. Nagel 1999, 36.
17. Barry 1973, 166.
18. Rawls's position is hardly unprecedented however. A significant cohort of late nineteenth and twentieth century liberals, including such prominent thinkers as J. S. Mill, T. H. Green, John Dewey, and others, offer a counterpoint to the laissez-faire or libertarian position. Building on these earlier writers, Rawls seeks in part to help codify this perspective by offering a surer philosophical foundation than earlier thinkers had provided.
19. As I argue further, this contention should not be mistaken for the claim that liberal principles require redistribution.
20. Pogge 1989, 10.
21. Rawls 2001, 7.
22. Alejandro 1998, 24.
23. Honig 1993, 129.
24. See e.g., Holmes 1995, where Rawls is described as "a defender of welfarist redistribution" (239).
25. Among the prominent critical voices raising this concern are Barber 1988; Honig 1993; Mouffe 1993; Benhabib 1996; Alejandro 1998; Bellamy 1999; and Waldron 1999b.
26. Rawls 1971, 7.
27. Nagel 1999, 36.
28. Rawls 2001, 64.
29. Ibid.
30. See Sandel 1984 for an especially insightful discussion of this aspect of Rawls's thought.
31. Rawls 1971, 11–12.
32. Rawls 2001, 42.
33. Ibid., 42–43.
34. Rawls 1971, 197.
35. Ibid., 198.

36. Ibid.
37. Ibid., 199.
38. Rawls 1993, 37.
39. Ibid., 175.
40. Ibid., 161.
41. Rawls 2001, 11–12.
42. Waldron 1999b, 151.
43. Bellamy 1999, 45.
44. Gray 2000, 75.
45. Alejandro 2000, 59.
46. Barber 1988, 57.
47. For two thoughtful efforts to understand the extent and nature of Rawls's commitment to democracy, see Cohen 2003 and Gutmann 2003.
48. Rawls 1993, 227.
49. Rawls 2001, 115.
50. Rawls 1971, 201.
51. Honig 1993, 127.
52. Rawls 2001, 41.
53. Ibid., 49.
54. While my claim that the vagueness of the two principles will lead to widespread debate can be only speculative, I am less hopeful than Rawls that constitutional questions will be regarded as settled based on the constitutional experience of the United States, which suggests that despite the presence of a generally revered constitution, constitutional challenges continuously arise in the courts and become especially heated during periods of broader social unrest.
55. For one of the earliest and best discussions of the indeterminacy of the two principles, see Hart 1975. See also Sandel's 1984 excellent discussion in *Liberalism and the Limits of Justice*.
56. Bellamy 1999, 53. See also Alejandro 1998, 58–59.
57. Waldron 1999a, 71.
58. Ironically, however, the very same critics who assail Rawls for emptying politics of meaningful content express outrage at the fact that Rawls refuses to presettle economic questions. Reflecting on the indeterminacy of the difference principle to resolve basic questions pertaining to the economic structure of the idea regime, Benjamin Barber 1988 declares that "a theory of justice that sees nothing to choose between capitalism and socialism is either extravagantly formalistic to the point of utter irrelevance, or it is a badly disguised rationalization for one particular socioeconomic system, namely, property-owning democracy" (81).

59. Rawls 1993, 166–167.
60. Ibid., 229.
61. Waldron 1999b, 157.
62. Rawls 1971, 198–199.
63. See Gillman 2001 and Dworkin 2002 for an engaging analyses of election 2000.
64. A similar argument can be made regarding Rawls's appropriation of the term "political." Waldron 1999b, 59 contends that "what is normally understood by politics is that it is an arena in which the members of some group debate and find ways of reaching decisions on various issues in spite of the fact that they disagree about the values and principles that the merits of those issues engage." Rawls's suggests that we view things differently. For him, politics is understood as an arena bounded by fundamental agreements in which people debate specifics within the context of shared agreements in principle.
65. Waldron 1999b, 71.
66. Rawls 2001, 50.
67. For a particularly strong criticism of Rawls on this point, see Honig 1993, 127. Honig emphasizes the extent to which "reconciliation, not politicization, is Rawls's goal in *A Theory of Justice*."
68. Rawls 1971, 201.
69. Ibid., 198.

Chapter Four   Liberalism's Legislative Renaissance

1. The term pluralism today conveys many meanings. Among political scientists, pluralism is often used to describe the view of U.S. politics as a system in which interest groups compete for limited resources. See Lowi 1979. For political philosophers, pluralism refers to the idea that the sources of value in human life are multiple and incommensurable. Larmore 1996 contends that liberalism properly understood is committed not to pluralism as a fact, but only to a recognition that reasonable people may disagree about fundamental matters of value. In other words, liberals can remain agnostic on the ultimate question of whether value is monistic or plural, recognizing that we lack the resources to arrive at an answer to this question. See pp. 152–174.
2. Bellamy 1999, 1.
3. Among the thinkers I would place in this camp are Richard Bellamy, Jeremy Waldron, and John Gray.

4. Gray 2000, 33.
5. Bellamy 1999, 3.
6. From the standpoint of liberal theory, provision for rights is typically understood as a way to designate limits on governmental power; rights mark a boundary beyond which government may not tread. While it is commonly assumed that rights must be constitutionalized to be respected, the U.S. case provides many examples which subvert this familiar view. Importantly, under the Constitution, legislators are endowed with the power to create rights through ordinary legislative acts, a fact that is easily obscured by the assumption that the Constitution itself is the sole bastion of rights. But consider the Civil Rights Act of 1964, e.g., which extends rights to victims of sex, gender, race, and other forms of discrimination far beyond anything described in the Constitution. In exercising their rights, most Americans don't pay much attention to whether these rights have their origins in Constitutional provisions or legislative actions, but there is of course one significant difference, namely, the relative ease with which legislatively established rights may be repealed.
7. For a particularly pointed challenge to legitimacy and effectiveness of judicial review, see Tushnet 1999.
8. The issue of terminology is especially difficult here. Ideally, the view I discuss would be referred to as "political liberalism," given the emphasis thinkers of this orientation place on the need for liberals to shift their focus from philosophical matters to political questions. However, Rawls appropriates the label "political liberalism" to describe his brand of liberalism, although he defines the term political in a very different way than I do—or as is customary amongst political theorists. For Rawls, the "political" in "political liberalism" is set in contrast to "metaphysical" accounts of justice that rest on more comprehensive forms of agreement than the overlapping consensus Rawls seeks. The thinkers I refer to here defend a liberalism that is "political" in a very different sense—"political" as opposed to "pre-settled" or "principled," that is, a liberalism in which politics proceeds not on the grounds of pre-settled agreements, but rather, in which politics generates the principles which constrain subsequent efforts at collective decision making. For the purposes of the discussion presented in this chapter, I use the term "pluralist liberalism" to designate the alternative approach adopted by Waldron and his ilk.
9. This is not to deny that some more traditional liberals also have acknowledged the shifting nature of rights in a liberal regime, but these real world departures from the ideal of pre-settled rights are typically treated as a regrettable effect of politics, one to be minimized as much as possible. Shklar seeks to finesse the problem that the instability of rights poses for an ideal of limited government based on a strict "prohibition upon invading the private

realm" with the insistence that "the important point for liberalism is not so much where the line is drawn, as that it be drawn, and that it must under no circumstances be ignored or forgotten" (1989, 24). See also Charney 1998, esp. p. 100.

10. Legal philosopher Ronald Dworkin is perhaps the most well-known contemporary defender of judicial review. However, it is interesting to note that Hayek is an exception in that he does not endorse judicial review as an essential feature of the ideal liberal regime. As discussed in chapter two, Hayek proposes a model constitution, the centerpiece of which is a plan to divide legislative power between two assemblies, the Governmental and the Legislative. Though Hayek also makes provision for a constitutional court with the power of judicial review, he anticipates that the division of legislative power he proposes will all but eliminate the need for such review by tying the hands of legislators before they act.

11. Rawls 1993, 213.

12. Ibid., 231.

13. Ibid., 233.

14. Ibid., 233.

15. Ibid., 235.

16. Cohen 2003, 120.

17. The phrase comes from Dworkin 1985. See also the discussion in Macedo 1990, 111–130.

18. Waldron 1999a, 2.

19. Ibid.

20. Campos 2000.

21. Waldron 1999b, 293–294.

22. Ibid., 109.

23. Ibid., 137.

24. Ibid., 55.

25. Ibid., 66.

26. Ibid., 220–221.

27. Ibid., 281.

28. While Waldron only mentions the U.S. framers in passing, Bellamy 1996 makes a parallel case regarding the U.S. founding, suggesting that Madison and Hamilton eschewed line-drawing in favor of a "republican" model of constitutionalism that relies centrally on the political process to produce limits on legislative power.

29. See pp. 9–11.

30. Waldron 1999b, 309.

31. Ibid.
32. Ibid.
33. Ibid.
34. Waldron 1999b, 310 quoting from Mill, *On Liberty*, Ch. 3, 90.
35. Waldron 1999a, 84.
36. Waldron 1999b, 307.
37. See Altman 1990 for an excellent introduction to the Critical Legal Studies movement.
38. Waldron 1999b, 66.
39. In reviews of Waldron's work, both Whittington and Posner contend that Waldron's theory proceeds in denial of the actual practice of legislative politics.
40. See Wolin 1993, 475.
41. James Madison, *The Federalist 10*, 54, in Issac Kramnick 1987.
42. Ibid., 58.
43. Ibid., 58–59.
44. See Epp 1998.
45. Waldron 1999b, 15.
46. See, e.g., Ackerman 1991, Whittington 1999, Griffin 1996, and Tushnet 1999.
47. Waldron 1999b, 290.
48. See Glendon 1991.
49. King 1998, 433. For more on jury nullification, see St. John 1997 and Abramson 1994.
50. The debate over jury nullification is complicated by the fact that it is difficult to determine how common a practice it is, given that juries are not required to provide an explanation for their decision when rendering a verdict. Some scholars suggest that the press has a tendency to exaggerate the frequency of nullification, particularly when considering high profile cases like the OJ Simpson murder trial, thereby contributing to a public sense that nullification powers are being abused and that steps must be taken to rein in runaway juries. See Marder 1999 for a more thorough discussion of the definition of nullification and an analysis of its recent deployment.

Chapter Five   Liberalism in the Age of Reality TV

1. Bellamy 1999, 10.
2. Ibid., 116.

3. Bellamy 1999, 121.

4. Barber 2001.

5. I am grateful to an anonymous reviewer of this manuscript for this formulation.

6. Dean 2000, 1. As Elizabeth Wingrove pointed out in offering comments on an earlier draft of this chapter, there is no reason to assume, as Dean seems to do, that the direction of causality moves only one way.

7. See Dean 2000. This book includes essays by some of the intellectual leaders in this arena of thought, a small but growing group of scholars.

8. According to a study conducted by the nonpartisan Committee for the Study of the American Electorate, 51.2% of eligible voters turned out for the 2000 presidential election, up slightly from 49% in 1996. (*New York Times*, August 31, 2001). Curtis Gans of the Center for the Study of the American Electorate reports a turnout of 59.6% of eligible citizens for the 2004 presidential election, the highest rate of turnout since 1968. See http://www.fairvote.org/ reports/CSAE2004electionreport.pdf.

9. At present, the term "reality TV" remains loosely defined among fans, the media, and scholars. In the subsequent section, I provide a more detailed discussion of the origins and characteristics of shows in this genre. For a comprehensive listing of shows popularly considered reality TV programs, visit www.sirlinksalot.com, one of the several websites devoted to the world of reality TV now flourishing on the internet.

10. See Miller and Shanks 1996, Piven 2000, Patterson 2002, and Wattenberg 2002.

11. See, e.g., Gans 1974, Levine 1988, Ross 1989, McGuigan 1992, and Grossberg 1992.

12. There are, of course, exceptions to the generally reverential tone with which voting is usually treated in the United States, including those political scientists who suggest that voting is irrational, or the Supreme Court's decision in *Bush v. Gore*, which emphasized, among other points, that there is no affirmative constitutional right to vote, but rather, only a right to have one's voice count as much (or as little) as everyone else's.

13. Jessica Silbey 2002. See also Sarat and Simon 2001 for a good overview of recent scholarship in this area.

14. Richard Sherwin 2000, 17.

15. In 2001, The Miss America Pageant announced a series of changes to its format broadcast from popular reality TV shows. The changes include allowing the 41 women who do not make the final cut to vote as an "eighth judge" for a winner of the competition; the creation of a "jury room" backstage, a

la shows like *Survivor* or *The Bachelor*, where non-finalists will talk about the finalists, and the inclusion of more audience interviews as part of the broadcast. See http://www.pressplus.com/missam/news/2001/tvtip.html.

16. "Campaign is the Ultimate Reality Show," *Los Angeles Times*, August 8, 2003, 1A. The article describes the election as "a reality TV show with a proven ratings winner cast as the star" and quotes one expert's observation that "It's entertaining. It's exciting. The circus has come to town. That's good for ratings." In an article appearing several days later under the heading "California Recall Reality Show: TV with no Producer," the author observes: "The recall itself has the air of a reality TV show, with a fresh twist." (*Los Angeles Times*, August 19, 2003 E1, E6).

17. MTV's popular series *The Real World*, which debuted in 1990, is often described as the first reality TV show.

18. Friedman 2002, 4–5. Although there remains a paucity of scholarly writing on reality TV, in recent years a small number of books have appeared which have begun to address some of the important social, political, and cultural issues raised by this emergent programming genre. See, e.g., Calvert 2000; Brenton and Cohen 2003.

19. See Gamson 1998.

20. For an insightful discussion of the shifting relationship between the ideas of fact and fiction in the postmodern age, see Linda Williams 1998. Contesting, as I do, the necessity of accepting a strictly binary relationship between fact and fiction, Williams contends that "instead of careening between idealistic faith in documentary truth and cynical recourse to fiction, we do better to define the documentary not as an essence of truth but as a set of strategies designed to choose from among a horizon or relative and contingent truths" (386).

21. See Varon 2004.

22. See Zizek 2002.

23. Ibid., 16.

24. Voting occurs at a variety of levels in a democracy, from mass voting for representatives to elite voting on the supreme court. For the purposes of my argument here, I am primarily interested in voting as it pertains to the selection of representatives. As an anonymous reviewer pointed out, there is also a potentially useful analogy to be drawn between voting on reality TV and voting that takes place in deliberative bodies like Congress. However, the voting dramas I focus on here are those which are built around the selection of persons, rather than policies.

25. See Isaac 1998.

26. Taking a related stand, political theorist Sheldon Wolin 1993 describes "electoral democracy" as a form of rule designed not to empower the people but rather to tame the passions of the demos by reducing civic participation to voting rights, a maneuver that "allows the citizenry to 'participate,' not in power but in the rituals and festivals of power."

27. This is very much a contemporary struggle. Disenfranchisement remains a reality for millions of U.S. citizens, especially those who have been convicted of felonies. According to the Washington-based think tank The Sentencing Project, 3.9 million Americans are subject to felony disenfranchisement, including 1 million persons who have completed their sentences. In the state of Florida, 1 out of 3 black men is disenfranchised, a fact that may have played a significant role in the outcome of the 2000 presidential election. For a more in-depth analysis, see the joint study published by Human Rights Watch and The Sentencing Project available online at http://www.hrw.org/reports98/vote/usvot98o.htm.

28. Apostolidis 2000.

29. During the winter 2003 season of *American Idol*, viewers were chastised midway through the competition by host Ryan Seacrest and the panel of judges for failing to cast responsible votes, and a stern reminder was issued that *American Idol* is a "talent show," not just a "popularity contest."

30. See Honig 2001.

31. See, e.g., Guinier 1995 and Disch 2002.

32. Notable exceptions include *Big Brother* and *American Idol*, both of which invite viewers to phone in votes to determine who gets to remain on the show.

33. See Ackerman and Fishkin 2004. See also Leib 2004.

34. Barber 1984, 188.

35. While the right to privacy is not questioned as it pertains to voting, in the next chapter I suggest that the social value of privacy is growing increasingly ambiguous.

36. I am indebted to Elizabeth Wingrove for offering this insight.

37. See the show's official website at http://www.sho.com/site/americancandidate/about_american. do. Originally owned by Rupert Murdoch's FX network, the show was dumped in May 2003 due to rising production costs. After HBO acquired the show only to drop its production plans after legal questions were raised by the FEC, Showtime finally made the decision to produce and air the show.

38. The winner of the competition was a social conservative named Park Gillespie. Many of his supporters were mobilized by Christian evangelical

groups, the Home School Legal Defense Association, and Focus on the Family.

39. Lisa de Moraes, *Washington Post*, September 21, 2002, C1.

40. See Brenton and Cohen 2003, 177.

41. "Crossing the Line for a Chance at Legal Status," *Los Angeles Times*, August 4, 2004, A1.

Chapter Six   A Liberal Future for Privacy Doctrine?

1. In recent years, a successful publishing niche has been carved out by authors who warn about the faltering state of privacy rights in the United States. Popular titles in this genre include Rosen 2000; Whittler 2000; Calls and Armacost 1997; and Brin 1999. Other signs of a privacy panic can be found in the recent willingness of legislators, at both the state and federal levels, to consider legislation that would curtail the rights of government and business to control personal information, including the Barr-Nadler bill compelling federal agencies to include a "privacy impact statement" on all proposals, and the recently defeated bill in California aimed at limiting corporate access to personal information.

2. Although as Kymlicka 1990 notes, liberals have meant different things by invoking the public/private divide at different times. See 247–262.

3. Allen 1999, 725.

4. http://www.access.gpo.gov/congress/icreport/. For the full text of the report, see Starr 1998.

5. In the popular discourse on privacy, a distinction is not always drawn between invasions of personal privacy emanating in state action and invasions originating in the acts of corporate or other "private" entities. For the purposes of the following discussion, I focus primarily on the former.

6. See e.g., Allen 1996, 1999; Boling 1996; and Cohen 1996, 1997.

7. See Pateman 1983 for a classic statement of the feminist position.

8. See e.g., Glendon 1987; Sandel 1996; and Etzioni 2000.

9. Holmes 1997, 255.

10. "Family of Three Dropping By, Along with Secret Service," *Los Angeles Times*, August 18, 1999.

11. In February 1997, a scandal arose when confidential White House memos revealed that President Clinton had personally authorized a plan to offer overnight stays in the Lincoln bedroom to potential party donors. The memos were released as part of a broader congressional investigation into Democratic

Party fund-raising practices following the 1996 election. See "Courting Donors: Clinton Pressed Plan to Reward Donors," by Alison Mitchell, New York Times A1.

12. Bezanson 1992, 1133.

13. Warren and Brandeis 1890.

14. Ibid.

15. Ibid.

16. *Griswold v. Connecticut*, 381 U.S. 479 (1965).

17. In this regard, it is interesting to consider the significance of the other major privacy case to arise in the 1960s, *Stanley v. Georgia* (1969). This case arose from the prosecution of a man charged with possession of obscene matter. The court found the Georgia statute prohibiting possession of such matter unconstitutional, thereby extending the right to privacy to cover individuals outside of the context of the marital relationship. Of course, to the extent that one agrees with law professor Catharine Mackinnon that the proliferation of pornography serves as an enabling condition for the perpetuation of the institution of marriage by creating a socially sanctioned space of transgression, this decision can be seen simply as an extension of the social logic underlying the *Griswold* decision.

18. *Griswold v. Connecticut*, 381 U.S. 479 (1965).

19. See, e.g., *Kelly v. Johnson,* 425 U.S. 238 (1976); *Moore v. City of East Cleveland,* 431 U.S. 494 (1977); and *Whalen v. Roe,* 429 U.S. 589 (1976).

20. Under the USA Patriot Act, passed shortly after the 9/11 attacks, Congress radically extended the surveillance power of law enforcement agencies under the guise of protecting national security. In the aftermath, immigrants, particularly those of middle eastern backgrounds, have been primary targets.

21. In June 2002, the Court held in *Board of Education of Independent School District No. 92 of Pottawatomie County vs. Earls* that public schools may subject high school students engaged in extracurricular activities to mandatory drug-testing.

22. Pateman 1989, 131.

23. Beinart 1999.

24. Elshtain 1997, 172.

25. For an argument urging feminists to abandon the privacy concept altogether, see Mackinnon 1987.

26. Weintraub and Krishan 1997, xi.

27. For a more extended consideration of the culture of publicity, see the discussion on reality TV in chapter five.

28. http://www.voyeurdorm.com

29. Rosen 2000.
30. See Feldman 2003.
31. *Poe v. Ullman*, 367 U.S. 497 (1961).
32. For an excellent discussion of these debates, see Kumar 1997.
33. This phenomenon is treated in greater detail in chapter five, where I consider the significance of the reality TV phenomenon.
34. Allen 1999.
35. Fishkin and Ackerman 2003, 7. For a more in-depth discussion of Deliberation Day, see Ackerman and Fishkin 2004.
36. Leib 2004, esp. 12–27.

REFERENCES

Abramson, Jeffrey. 1994. *We the jury: The jury system and the ideal of democracy*. Cambridge: Harvard University Press.

Ackelsberg, Martha and Mary Lyndon Shanley. 1996. Privacy, publicity, and power: A feminist rethinking of the public-private distinction. In *Revisioning the political: Feminist reconstructions of traditional concepts in western political theory*. Edited by Nancy Hirschmann and Christine Di Stefano. New York: Westview Press, 213–234.

Ackerman, Bruce. 1991. *We the people: Foundations*. Cambridge MA: Harvard University Press.

——. 1996. The Political Case for constitutional courts. In *Liberalism without illusions*. Edited by Bernard Yack. Chicago: University of Chicago Press.

Ackerman, Bruce and James S. Fishkin. 2003. Deliberation day. In *Debating deliberative democracy*. Edited by James S. Fishkin and Peter Laslett. New York: Blackwell Publishing.

——. 2004. *Deliberation day*. New Haven CT: Yale University Press.

Alejandro, Roberto. 1998. *The limits of Rawlsian justice*. Baltimore MD: Johns Hopkins University Press.

Allen, Anita. 1996. Privacy at home: A Twofold problem. In *Revisioning the political: Feminist reconstructions of traditional concepts in western political theory*. Edited by Nancy Hirschmann and Christine Di Stefano. New York: Westview Press, 193–212.

——. 1999. Coercing privacy. *William and Mary Law Review* 40(3): 723–758.

Altman, Andrew. 1990. *Critical legal studies*. Princeton NJ: Princeton University Press.

Apostolidis, Paul. 2000. Action or distraction? Cultural studies in the United States. In *Cultural studies & political theory*. Edited by Jodi Dean. Ithaca NY: Cornell University Press, 147–166.

Barber, Benjamin. 1984. *Strong democracy: Participatory democracy for a new age.* Los Angeles: University of California Press.

———. 1988. *The conquest of politics: Liberal philosophy in democratic times.* Princeton: Princeton University Press.

Barber, Sotirios. 1997. *The constitution of judicial power.* Baltimore: Johns Hopkins University Press.

Barry, Brian. 1973. *The liberal theory of justice.* Oxford: Clarendon Press.

———. 1989. *The conquest of politics: Liberal philosophy in democratic times.* Princeton NJ: Princeton University Press.

———. 2001. *Why liberals can't be strong democrats (and it's a good thing too).* Presented at the American Political Science Association Meeting in San Francisco, Aug 30–Sept 2.

Beinart, Peter. 1999. How the personal became political. *New Republic* (February): 21.

Bellamy, Richard. 1992. *Liberalism and modern society.* University Park PA: Pennsylvania State University Press.

———. 1994. Dethroning politics: Liberalism, constitutionalism, and democracy in the thought of F. A. Hayek. *British Journal of Political Science* 24: 419–441.

———. 1996. The political form of the constitution: The separation of powers, rights, and representative democracy. *Political Studies* XLIV: 437–457.

———. 1999. *Liberalism and pluralism: Towards a politics of compromise.* New York: Routledge.

Benhabib, Seyla. 1996. Toward a deliberative model of democratic legitimacy. In *Democracy and difference: Contesting the boundaries of the political.* Edited by Seyla Benhabib. Princeton NJ: Princeton University Press, 67–94.

Bezanson, Randall. 1992. "The right to privacy" revisited: Privacy, news, and social change, 1890–1990. *California Law Review* 80: 1133–1176.

Bickel, Alexander. [1962] 1986. *The least dangerous branch: The supreme court at the bar of politics.* New Haven: Yale University Press.

Boling, Patricia. 1996. *Privacy and the politics of intimate life.* Ithaca NY: Cornell University Press.

Brenton, Sam and Reuben Cohen. 2003. *Shooting people: Adventures in reality tv.* New York: Verso.

Brin, David. 1999. *The transparent society: Will technology force us to choose between privacy and freedom?* New York: Perseus.

Burchell, Graham, Colin Gordon, and Peter Miller. 1991. *The Foucault effect: Studies in governmentality.* Chicago: University of Chicago Press.

Caldwell, Bruce. 2003. *Hayek's challenge: An intellectual biography of F. A. Hayek.* Chicago: University of Chicago Press.

Calls, Fred and Michael Armacost. 1997. *Privacy in the information age.* Washington DC: The Brookings Institution.

Calvert, Clay. 2000. *Voyeur nation.* New York: Westview Press.

Campos, Paul. 2000. *Jurismania: The madness of American law.* New York: Oxford University Press.

Casper, Gerhard. 1996. *Separating powers: Essays on the founding period.* Cambridge MA: Harvard University Press.

Charney, Evan. 1998. Political liberalism, deliberative democracy, and the public sphere. *American Political Science Review* 92(1): 97–110.

Cohen, Jean L. 1996. Democracy, difference, and the right of privacy. In *Democracy and difference: Contesting the boundaries of the political.* Edited by Seyla Benhabib. Princeton NJ: Princeton University Press, 187–217.

———. 1997. Rethinking privacy: Autonomy, identity, and the abortion controversy. In *Public and private in thought and practice.* Edited by Jeff Weintraub and Krishan Kumar. Chicago: University of Chicago Press, 133–165.

Cohen, Joshua. 2003. For a democratic society. In *The Cambridge companion to Rawls.* Edited by Samuel Freeman. New York: Cambridge University Press, 86–138.

Cowart, Lisa. 1998. Legislative prerogative v. judicial discretion: California's three strikes law takes a hit. *DePaul Law Review* 47: 615.

Dahl, Robert A. 1989. *Democracy and its critics.* New Haven CT: Yale University Press.

Dean, Jodi. 2000. Introduction: The interface of political theory and cultural studies. In *Cultural studies and political theory.* Edited by Jodi Dean. Ithaca: Cornell University Press, 1–22.

Disch, Lisa. 2002. *The tyranny of the two party system.* New York: Columbia University Press.

Dworkin, Ronald. 1985. The forum of principle. In *A matter of principle.* Cambridge MA: Harvard University Press, 33–71.

———, ed. 2002. *A badly flawed election: Debating Bush v. Gore, the supreme court, and American democracy.* New York: The New Press.

Ebenstein, Alan. 2003. *Hayek's journey: The mind of Friedrich Hayek.* New York: Palgrave.

Elshtain, Jean Bethke. 1996. The displacement of politics. In *Public and private in thought and practice: Perspectives on a grand dichotomy.* Edited by Jeff Weintraub and Krishan Kumar. Chicago: University of Chicago Press, 166–181.

Epp, Charles R. 1998. *The rights revolution: Lawyers, activists and supreme courts in comparative perspective.* Chicago: Chicago University Press.

Etzioni, Amitai. 2000. *The limits of privacy.* New York: Basic Books.

Ewick, Patricia and Susan S. Silbey. 1998. *The common place of law*. Chicago: University of Chicago Press.

Feldman, Leonard. 2003. *The home ideal and democratic theory*. Paper presented at the Western Political Science Association Meeting. Denver, CO.

Flathman, Richard. 1994. Liberalism and the suspect enterprise of political institutionalization: The case of the rule of law. In *NOMOS XXXVI: The rule of law*. Edited by Ian Shapiro. New York: New York University Press.

Friedman, James, ed. 2002. *Reality squared: Televisual discourse on the real*. New Brunswick NJ: Rutgers University Press.

Gamble, Andrew. 1996. *Hayek: The iron cage of liberty*. New York: Westview Press.

Gamson, Joshua. 1998. *Freaks talk back*. Chicago: University of Chicago Press.

Gans, Herbert. 1974. *Popular culture and high culture*. New York: Basic Books.

Gillman, Howard. 2001. *The votes that counted: How the court decided the 2000 presidential election*. Chicago: University of Chicago Press.

Glendon, Mary Ann. 1987. *Abortion and divorce in western law*. Cambridge MA: Harvard University Press.

——. 1991. *The impoverishment of political discourse*. New York: Simon & Schuster.

Gordon, Colin. 1991. Governmental rationality: An introduction. In *The Foucault effect*. Edited by Burchell et al. Chicago: University of Chicago Press.

Gray, John. 1982. F.A. Hayek and the rebirth of classical liberalism. *Literature of Liberty* 5: 1–105.

——. 1984. *Hayek on liberty*. London: Oxford University Press.

——. 2000. *Two faces of liberalism*. New York: The New Press.

Griffin, Stephen M. 1996. *American constitutionalism: From theory to politics*. Princeton: Princeton University Press.

Grossberg, Lawrence. 1992. *We gotta get out of this place*. New York: Routledge.

Guinier, Lani. 1995. *The tyranny of the majority*. New York: The Free Press.

Gutmann, Amy. 1996. How limited is liberal government?. In *Liberalism without illusions*. Edited by Bernard Yack. Chicago: University of Chicago Press.

——. 2003. Rawls on the relationship between liberalism and democracy. In *The Cambridge companion to Rawls*. Edited by Samuel Freeman. New York: Cambridge University Press, 168–199.

Hamilton, Alexander, John Jay, and James Madison. [1788] 2000. *The federalist*. Edited with an Introduction by Robert Scigliano. New York: Random House.

Hamowy, Ronald. 1961. Hayek's concept of freedom: a critique. *New Individualist Review* I: 28–31.

——. 1978. Law and the liberal society: F. A. Hayek's constitution of liberty. *Journal of Libertarian Studies* 2(4): 287–297.

———. 1982. The Hayekian model of government in an open society. *Journal of Libertarian Studies* 6: 137–143.

Hart, H. L. A. 1975. Rawls on liberty and its priority. In *Reading Rawls*. Edited by Norman Daniels. Oxford: Blackwell Press, 230–252.

Hayek, Friedrich A. [1944] 1976. *The road to serfdom*. Chicago: University of Chicago Press.

———. 1945. The uses of knowledge in society. *The American Economic Review* 35(4): 519–530.

———. [1960] 1978. *The constitution of liberty*. Chicago: University of Chicago Press.

———. 1961. Freedom and coercion: some comments and Mr. Hamowy's criticism. *New Individualist Review* 1: 28–31.

———. 1973. *Law legislation and liberty, vol. 1: Rules and order*. Chicago: Chicago University Press.

———. 1976. *Law legislation and liberty, vol. 2: The mirage of social justice*. Chicago: Chicago University Press.

———. 1979. *Law legislation and liberty, vol. 3: The political order of a free people*. Chicago: Chicago University Press.

Holmes, Stephen. 1995. *Passions and constraint: On the theory of liberal democracy*. Chicago: University of Chicago Press.

Honig, Bonnie. 1993. *Political theory and the displacement of politics*. Ithaca: Cornell University Press.

———. 2001. *Democracy and the foreigner*. Princeton: Princeton University Press.

Isaac, Jeffrey. 1998. *Democracy in dark times*. Ithaca: Cornell University Press.

King, Nancy. 1998. Silencing nullification: Advocacy inside the jury room and outside the courtroom. *University of Chicago Law Review* 65: 433.

Kramnick, Isaac. 1987. Editor's introduction. *The Federalist papers*. New York: Penguin.

Kresge Stephen and Leif Wenar, eds. 1994. *Hayek on Hayek*. Chicago: University of Chicago Press.

Kukathas, Chandran. 1990. *Hayek and modern liberalism*. London: Oxford University Press.

Kumar, Krishan. 1997. The promise and predicament of private life at the end of the twentieth century. In *Public and private in thought and practice: Perspectives on a grand dichotomy*. Edited by Jeff Weintraub and Krishan Kumar. Chicago: University of Chicago Press, 204–236.

Kymlicka, Will. 1990. *Contemporary political philosophy: An introduction*. New York: Oxford University Press.

Larmore, Charles. 1996. *The morals of modernity*. New York: Cambridge University Press.

Leib, Ethan J. 2004. *Deliberative democracy in America: A proposal for a popular branch of government*. University Park PA: Pennsylvania University Press.

Levine, Lawrence. 1988. *Highbrow/lowbrow: The emergence of cultural hierarchy in America*. Cambridge: Harvard University Press.

Locke, John. 1960. Two treatises of Government. Edited by Peter Laslett. New York: Cambridge University Press.

Lowi, Theodore. 1979. *The end of liberalism*. 2nd edition. New York: W.W. Norton.

——. 1996. *The end of the republican era*. Norman OK: The University of Oklahoma Press.

Macedo, Stephen. 1990. *Liberal virtues: Citizenship, virtue, and community in liberal constitutionalism*. Oxford: Clarendon Press.

Mackinnon, Catharine. 1987. Privacy v. equality. In *Feminism Unmodified*. Cambridge MA: Harvard University Press.

Marder, Nancy J. 1999. The myth of the nullifying Jury. Northwestern University Law Review. 93: 877–959.

McGuigan, Jim. 1992. *Cultural populism*. New York: Routledge.

Mill, John Stuart. 1975. *On Liberty*. Edited by Gertrude Himmelfarb. New York: Penguin Books.

Miller, Warren and J. Merrill Shanks. 1996. *The new American voter*. Cambridge MA: Harvard University Press.

Mouffe, Chantal. 1993. *The return of the political*. New York: Verso.

Nagel, Thomas. 1999. The rigorous compassion of John Rawls: Justice, justice, shalt thou pursue. *The New Republic*, Oct 25, 1999.

Newey, Glen. 2001. *After politics: The rejection of politics in contemporary liberal philosophy*. New York: Palgrave.

Newmann, Stephen. 1984. *Liberalism at wits' end: The libertarian revolt against the modern state*. Ithaca NY: Cornell University Press.

Norton, Anne. 1993. *Republic of signs: Liberal theory and American popular culture*. Chicago: University of Chicago Press.

Nozick, Robert. 1989. *The examined life*. New York: Simon and Schuster.

Olsen, Frances. 1991. A finger to the devil: Abortion, privacy and equality. *Dissent* (summer): 377–382.

Pateman, Carole. 1983. Feminist critiques of the public/private dichotomy. *In Public and Private in Social Life*. Edited by S. I. Benn and G. F. Gaus. London: Croom Helm.

——. 1989. *The disorder of women*. Palo Alto CA: Stanford University Press.

Patterson, Thomas E. 2000. *The vanishing voter: Public involvement in an age of uncertainty*. New York: Knopf.

Piven, Frances Fox. 2000. *Why Americans still don't vote*. Boston: Beacon Press.

Pogge, Thomas. 1989. *Realizing Rawls*. Ithaca NY: Cornell University Press.

Posner, Richard A. 2000. Book Review: Review of Jeremy Waldron, Law and Disagreement. *Columbia Law Review* 100: 582–592.

Rakove, Jack. 1996. *Original meanings: Politics and ideas in the making of the constitution*. New York: Vintage Books.

———. 1998. *Declaring rights: A brief history with documents*. New York: Bedford Books.

Rawls, John. 1963. Constitutional liberty and the concept of justice. In *NOMOS VI: Justice*. New York: Atherton Press.

———. 1971. *A theory of justice: Revised edition*. Cambridge MA: Harvard University Press.

———. 1993. *Political liberalism*. New York: Columbia University Press.

———. 2001. *Justice as fairness: A restatement*. Cambridge MA: Harvard University Press.

Richardson, Henry. 2002. *Democratic autonomy: Public reasoning about the ends of policy*. New York: Oxford University Press.

Riker, William. [1982] 1988. *Liberalism against populism: A confrontation between the theory of democracy and the theory of social choice*. Prospect Heights IL: Waveland Press, Inc.

Rosen, Jeffrey. 2000. *The unwanted gaze: The destruction of privacy in America*. New York: Random House.

Ross, Andrew. 1989. *No respect: Intellectuals and popular culture*. New York: Routledge.

Sandel, Michael. 1984. *Liberalism and the limits of justice*. New York: Cambridge University Press.

———. 1996. *Democracy's discontent: America in search of a public philosophy*. Cambridge MA: Harvard University Press.

Sarat, Austin and Jonathan Simon. 2001. Beyond legal realism?: Cultural analysis, cultural studies, and the situation of legal scholarship. *Yale Journal of Law and Humanities* 13(3): 3–32.

Scheuerman, William. 1997. The unholy alliance of Carl Schmitt and Friedrich A. Hayek. *Constellations* IV: 172–188.

Sherwin, Richard. 2000. *When law goes pop: The vanishing line between law and popular culture*. Chicago: University of Chicago Press.

Shklar, Judith. 1989. The Liberalism of fear. In *Liberalism and the Moral Life*. Edited by Nancy L. Rosenblum. Cambridge MA: Harvard University Press.

Silbey, Jessica. 2002. What we do when we do law and popular culture. *Law & Social Inquiry* 27 (Winter): 139.

St. John, Richard. 1997. Note: Licence to nullify—the democratic and constitutional deficiencies of authorized jury lawmaking. *Yale Law Journal* 106(8): 2563–2597.

Starr, Kenneth. 1998. *The Starr report: The findings of independent counsel Kenneth Starr on President Clinton and the Lewinsky affair.* New York: Public Affairs.

Sunstein, Cass. 1996. *Political reasoning and moral conflict.* New York: Oxford University Press.

Tushnet, Mark. 1999. *Taking the constitution away from the courts.* Princeton: Princeton University Press.

Varon, Jeremy. 2004. It was the spectacle stupid: The Clinton-Lewinsky-Starr affair and the politics of the gaze. *In Public affairs: Politics in the age of sex scandals.* Edited by Paul Apostolidis and Juliet Williams. Durham NC: Duke University Press.

Wainwright, Hilary. 1994. *Arguments for a new left: Answering the free-market right.* New York: Blackwell.

Waldron, Jeremy. 1993. *Liberal rights: Collected papers 1981–1991.* New York: Cambridge University Press.

——. 1999a. *The dignity of legislation.* New York: Cambridge University Press.

——. 1999b. *Law and disagreement.* New York: Oxford University Press.

Warren, Samuel and Louis D. Brandeis. 1890. The right to privacy. *Harvard Law Review* 4(5): 193–220.

Wattenberg, Martin. 2002. *Where have all the voters gone?* Cambridge MA: Harvard University Press.

Weintraub, Jeff. 1997. The theory and politics of the public/private distinction. In *Public and private in thought and practice: Perspectives on a grand dichotomy.* Edited by Jeff Weintraub and Krishan Kumar. Chicago: Chicago University Press, 1–42.

Whittington, Keith. 1999. *Constitutional construction: Divided powers and constitutional meaning.* Cambridge MA: Harvard University Press.

——. 2000. In defense of legislatures (review essay). *Political Theory* 28(5): 690–702.

Whittler, Reg. 2000. *The end of privacy: How total surveillance is becoming a reality.* New York: The New Press.

Williams, Juliet. 2004. On what a constitution is—and isn't. In *After national democracy: Rights, law, and power in America and the new Europe.* Edited by Lars Tragardh. New York: Hart Publishing, 105–120.

Williams, Linda. 1998. Mirrors without memories: Truth, history, and the thin blue line. In *Documenting the Documentary.* Edited by Barry Keith Grant and Jeanette Slonioswski. Detroit MI: Wayne State University Press, 379–396.

Wills, Gary. 1999. *A necessary evil: A history of American distrust of government*. New York: Simon & Schuster.

Wolin, Sheldon. 1993. Democracy: Electoral and athenian. *PS: Political Science & Politics* 26(3): 475–478.

———. 1996. Fugitive democracy. In *Democracy and difference: Contesting the boundaries of the political*. Edited by Seyla Benhabib. Princeton NJ: Princeton University Press, 31–45.

Wood, Gordon. 1969. *The creation of the American republic 1776–1787*. Chapel Hill NC: University of North Carolina Press.

Young, Iris Marion. 1990. *Justice and the politics of difference*. Princeton: Princeton University Press.

Zizek, Slavoj. 2002. *Welcome to the desert of the real*. New York: Verso.

INDEX